Workbook
for
Imam al-Ghazali
The Book of Knowledge
for Children

-subhanahu wa ta ala: Glory be to He

-salla-llahu alayhi wa sallam: Peace and blessings be upon him

-alayhi-s-salam: Be upon him peace

-alayha-s-salam: Peace be upon her.

-radia-llahu anhu: May God be pleased with him

Dear Children, Families, and Teachers,

There is something for each age group in the pages to follow. Parents can simplify the questions and activities for the very small; some of you might like to color; others can do the questions and activities on their very own. Comics are provided in the back of the workbook for older children, along with ideas for further activities and a school curriculum.

Everyone is invited to the website: ghazalichildren.org to meet with your global brothers and sisters, to participate in contests, to submit your own ideas for activities, for curriculum, updates, and anything else. Simply enjoy the many resources provided and join in on a regular basis.

The Publisher

Workbook
for
Imam al-Ghazali
The Book of Knowledge
for Children

FONS VITAE

First published in 2016 by
Fons Vitae
49 Mockingbird Valley Drive
Louisville, KY 40207
http://www.fonsvitae.com
Email: fonsvitaeky@aol.com

Library of Congress Control Number 2015956970

ISBN 978-1941610-190

Printed in China

Illustrations by Fritz Hilton
Comics by Farida Khalil
line drawings by Liz Swearingen and Natalio G. Alob, Jr.,
and a painting by Cara Helminski

Cover by Gwen Burke

Please frequent www.ghazalichildren.org for updates,
competitions, meeting one another and much more.

Table of Contents

The Life of Imam al-Ghazali

A long time ago, nearly a thousand years, there lived a poor family in a town called Tus. The father wove cloth on a loom to support the family.

One day, they were blessed to have a son whom they named Muhammad, which means "the Praised one."

Muhammad was sent to take lessons from a wise elder in Tus, who was a good and honorable man; all that he did and said was beautiful!

Soon Muhammad and his brother Ahmed went to another school in nearby Nishapur. There they had a truly great and intelligent teacher named Imam al-Juwayni, who was also blessed to have such fine pupils as these two lads.

Muhammad al-Ghazali was a careful student and wrote down all that the teacher was saying, placing these notes in a bundle which he could carry with him.

One day, on the road home from Nishapur where he had continued his studies, thieves came upon his caravan. He was afraid they would steal his precious treasure: the many lessons he had copied and safely kept.

All the other travelers were robbed of their valuables. When they snatched away young Muhammad's notes, thinking it was something of great value, Muhammad cried out, "Oh please, don't take my bundle!"

The thieves ransacked the package, throwing papers in all directions! They asked the young pupil, "Of what use are these pages?"

The terrified boy pleaded and replied, "If you destroy all my notes from my lessons, I will be ruined! I have worked so hard to record all I was being taught by my teachers!"

One thief said, "All you know is written on papers and can so easily be taken away from you? What kind of knowledge is THAT?!?"

At that moment, young Muhammad al-Ghazali realized that true knowledge has to become part of you – the way you live and act! From this scary event with the thieves, he learned a huge lesson which changed his whole life.

Later, when Muhammad grew up, he was so intelligent that he became a truly great teacher himself. He knew more than anyone else and he spoke so beautifully that both students and other teachers crowded in to hear his lessons.

If anyone argued with Imam Muhammad al-Ghazali, he always won because he was smarter than <u>everyone</u>!!! He spoke both the Persian and Arabic languages well. People were amazed and dazzled by his brilliance.

As Imam al-Ghazali continued to give his lessons and lectures at the great Nizamiyya University, in the city of Baghdad, he began to grow very sad and upset! He noticed that he was very proud of himself, and very "puffed up"!

He watched himself think, "I am better and smarter than everyone else!"

This made him deeply worried about his own heart, because he knew that the very things he was teaching to others in his classes, he wasn't even doing himself.

He was teaching others that Allah ﷻ wants us all to be humble and NOT puffed-up and proud. The Imam's lessons were about how short our lives are and how we have to get ourselves ready and good enough to go on to our next life and home in Paradise. He was telling students NOT to be "hypocrites."

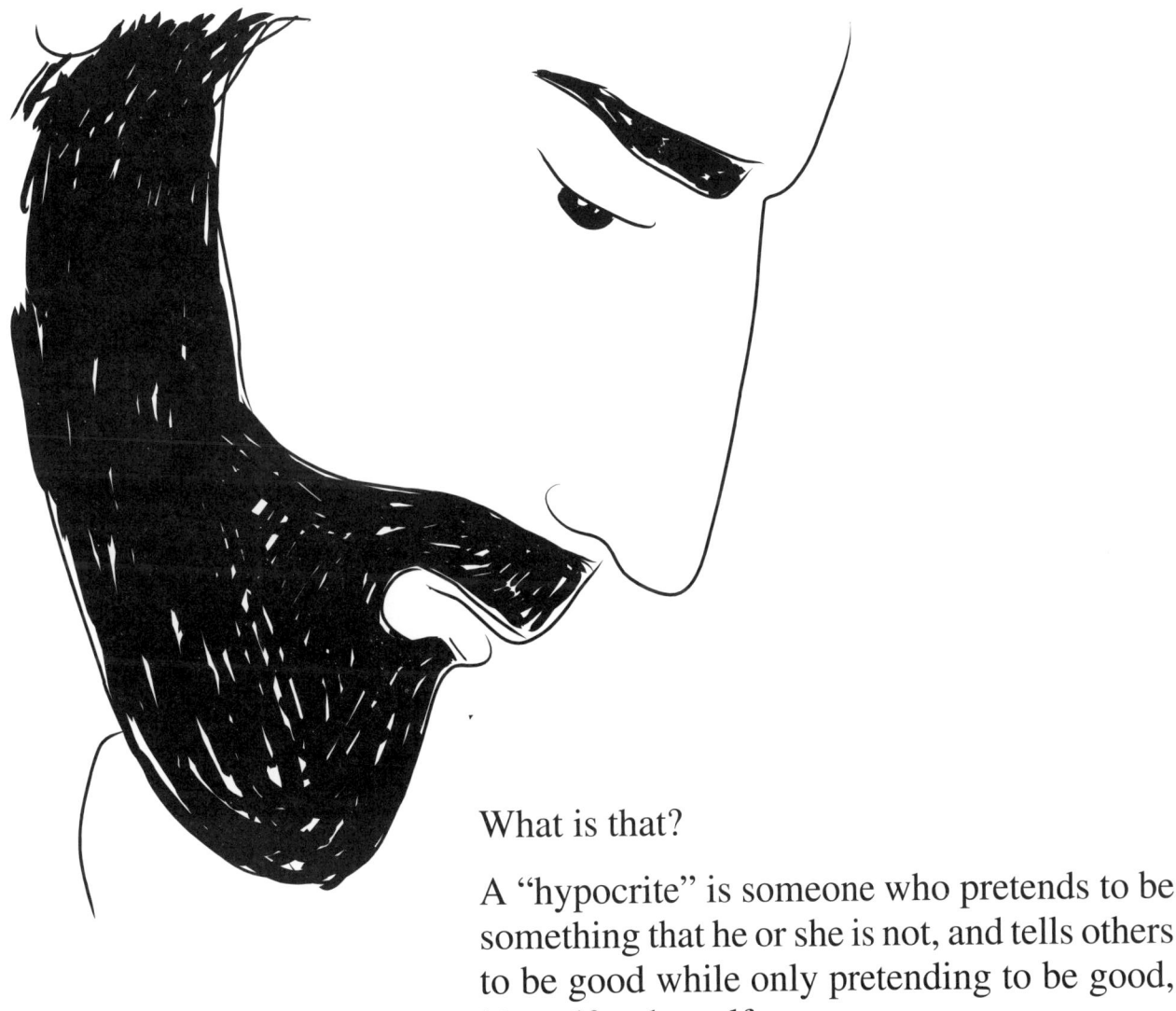

What is that?

A "hypocrite" is someone who pretends to be something that he or she is not, and tells others to be good while only pretending to be good, himself or herself.

In his heart he knew that he should give up his easy life and his job, where he enjoyed being so famous, and find a way to be humble and to polish his own Heart before he died. In that way he could best serve others because he would be a living example of the truths he was teaching rather then simply talking about these truths.

He exclaimed, "I am on the edge of a crumbling bank, and if I don't leave now, when will I get away from wasting my life by being untrue to myself? When will I start my journey to Paradise instead of just having good times and teaching others that they should reach a beautiful state of being which I am not even doing myself?"

But he loved his life and his fame too much, and he continued going to teach at the university. Then, one day, Allah ﷻ helped the Imam, through His love and mercy.

God ﷻ knew that the Imam had a good and pure Heart, but was too weak to abandon his way of life and leave the place where he was so important and admired by everyone.

So, when Imam al-Ghazali went to the school the next day and was about to begin to teach, God ﷻ blessed him . . . by taking away his voice! Not one word came out! The Imam was embarrassed and confused!

The doctors found that his body was not sick, but that his good soul was deeply troubled. The Imam knew inside his Heart that he needed to leave the life he was trapped in, and go in search of God ﷾.

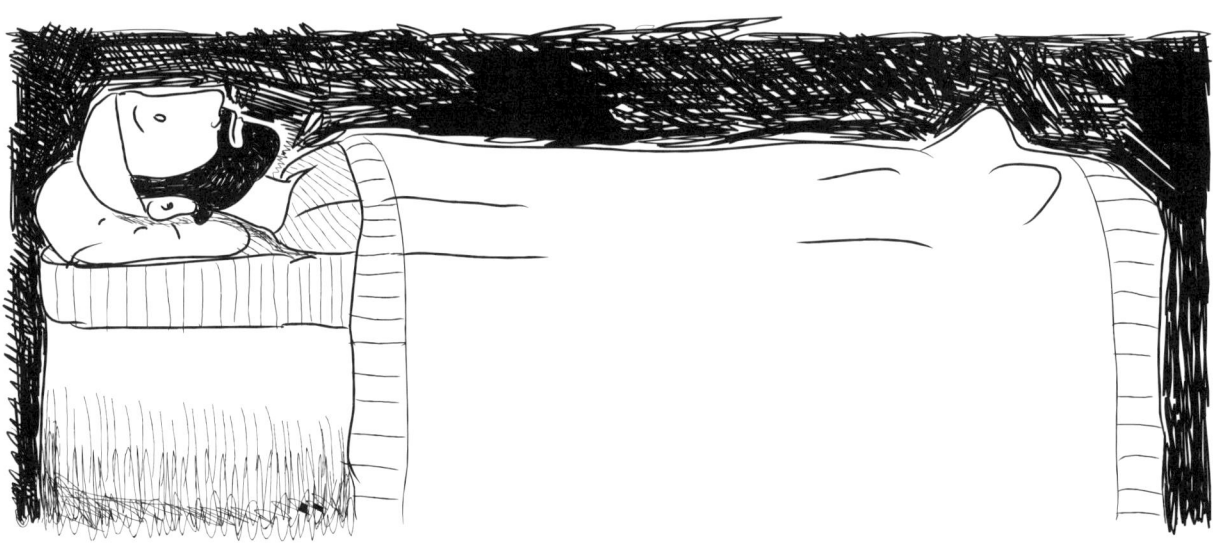

So he made arrangements for his family and left to seek the treasure of REAL knowledge—holy spiritual divine learning—not just learning for the everyday life.

In Damascus, he found a job cleaning the floor of the mosque, and he found that, even when he was tempted to share his great knowledge with others, he held back. He didn't let himself be better than others. He didn't show off any more.

He traveled to Jerusalem and to the holy city of Mecca where he sat in the company of great and wise Muslims. He learned much from their example.

No longer did he just KNOW all ABOUT Islam, but his heart was being filled to the brim with goodness and peace. During his journey he was writing the books which explained the deeper meanings of everything in his religion. He gave all of us a great, great gift today by showing us that we aren't just being given rules to follow. Imam al-Ghazali wrote for us all about inner beauty and meaning of these rules and practices we do, and showed that these are beautiful ways to help us along our way back to God ﷻ, Who created us and everything in the world!

Finally, he returned home for good, to his wife and daughters. We are very blessed that he explained for us what our lives really are for and what good and joyful things we get to do each day in order to become nearer to and loved by God ﷾.

Ameen, O Lord!

Questions About Imam al-Ghazali's Life

1. Who was Imam al-Ghazali and how long ago did he live?

2. When he was a teacher, what <u>bad</u> things did he notice about himself. (Check the correct boxes.)

___Not friendly	___Lazy
___Full of himself with Pride	___Selfish
___Jealous	___A Liar
___Mean	___A thief

3. What happened to him one day when he was teaching that changed his life?

4. Where did he go after he made good arrangements for his family?

5. What did the Imam learn on his journey?

6. Before and after he came home, what kinds of books did he write?

Fons Vitae hopes you will enjoy this workbook created to accompany your "Book of Knowledge." We have tried to provide things to do for all ages. Some exercises are for young children, and others—such as the comics—are for older. Included also is a Curriculum Manual for Teachers and Parents which provides suggestions for a variety of activities and games for both school and home. We have found that both the book and workbook have actually proven very useful for grown-ups in their own spiritual lives.

An interactive website has been created for announcements of competitions, updates of curriculum, postings from the community, the downloading of e-book versions of the Series (www.GhazaliChildren.org), and as a venue for children, their parents, and teachers from all over the Muslim world to meet one another and exchange ideas.

"We are taught to seek knowledge even if it comes from China."

Chapter 1
Two Kinds of Learning

1. One kind of learning helps you in your everyday life. Name three things you have learned about how to take care of your body.

a.   b.   c.

2. How does learning math, how to add and subtract, help you?

3. The other higher special learning teaches you how to polish your Shining Heart. Name something you have learned that will help you go to Paradise in the Next Life.

4. What books can teach you the higher Special Learning?

5. What are the two kinds of hearts that you have?

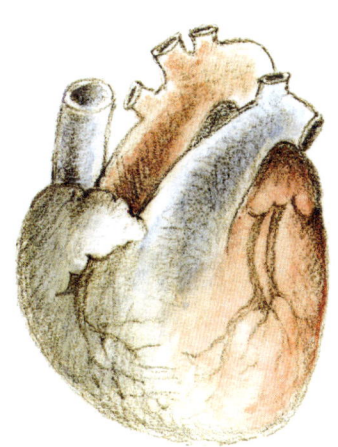   

6. Make up and play a game and act out one good thing you do. For example: Play that you are having fun sharing your toys. Then play how mean you are, when you won't share. Ask your parents to pretend not to share. What do you feel inside when you see them refusing to share?

In what way are people better than animals? The elephant is bigger and the camel is stronger.

Chapter 2
Animals and People

1. Describe some amazing things that you notice about animals! What is special about birds?

2. Pretend you are a cat or bird. What is it like? What might the cat be thinking about? What could the bird be thinking? What have you been thinking?

3. What makes people extra special? What can we learn that a cat or bird cannot?

4. Name some things that you feed your body? What kind of "food" does your Heart need?

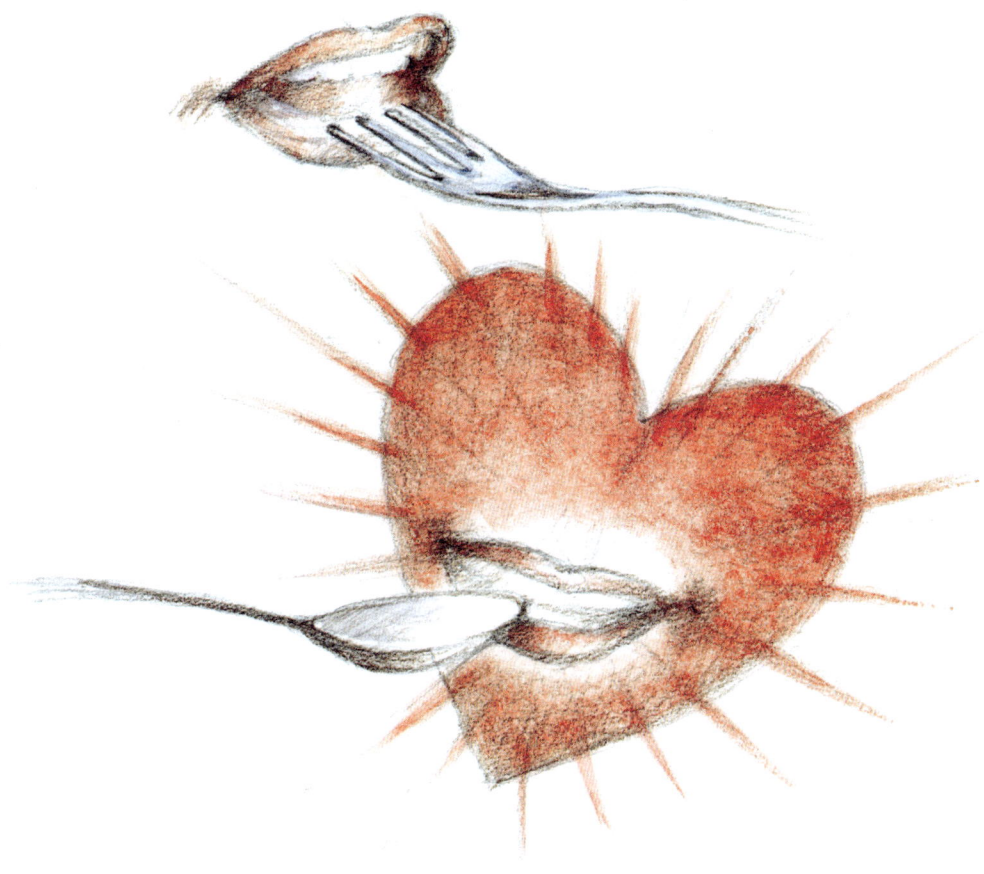

If you are going on a journey, don't you prepare what you need to take?

Chapter 3
The Two Worlds

1. Draw or describe some beautiful things in this world which God ﷻ made. Can you draw the sun? A tree? What else?

2. Pretend you are going on a camping trip with your family. What would you like to take with you? What will you pack?

a.

b.

3. What kinds of things do you need to learn in *this* world in order to be able to go to the Next World, which is even more beautiful than this world?

a.

b.

4. To get ready to travel to the Next World, what are some ways you can be? What can you BE like, what sort of a person? Circle the right ones:

Kind	Lazy	Bad Moods	Helpful
Sharing	Joyful	Naughty	Angry

What doesn't sink if your boat tips over? Only ONE thing won't sink and get lost. What is that?

Chapter 4
How to Enter The Garden

1. On the picture of the tipped-over boat, draw in a few of your own toys that will sink to the bottom of the river.

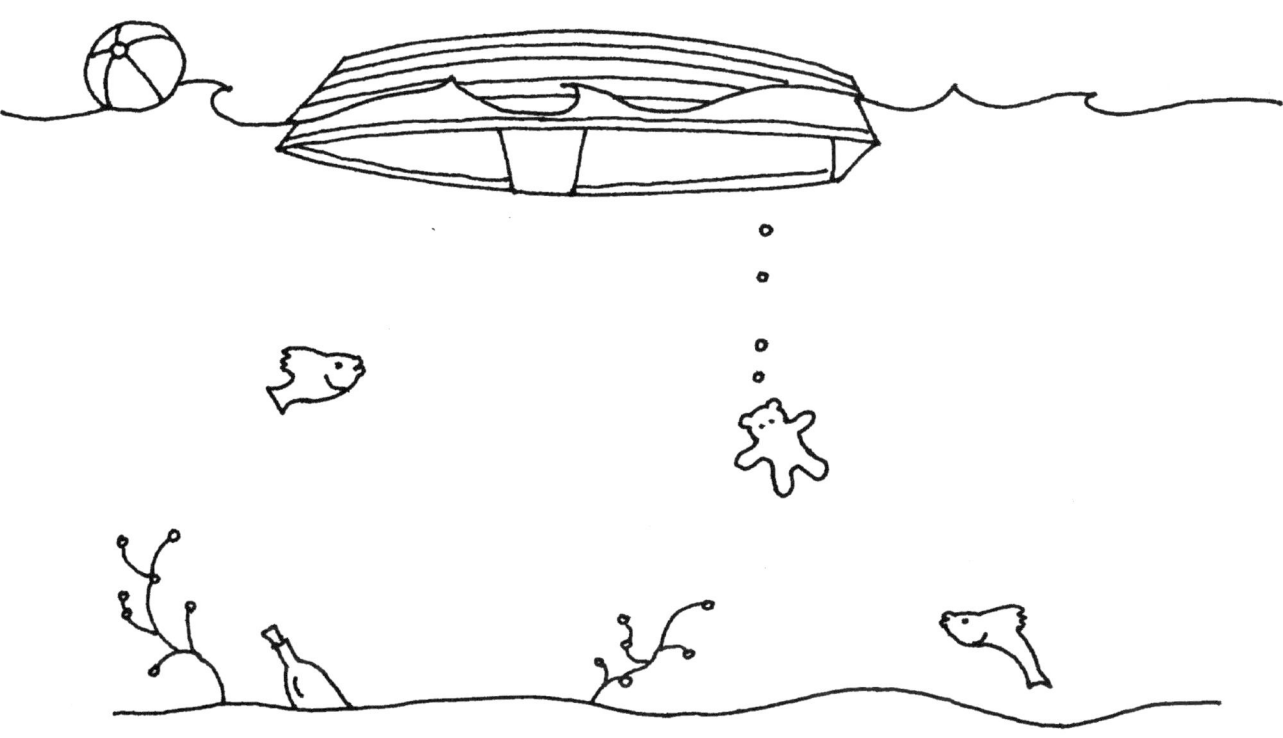

2. If your boat tips over, all your toys will sink to the bottom. But all the good that your shining Heart has done will NOT sink! Name some good things you have learned that you CAN take with you to the Next World.

    a.   b.

    c.   d.

3. Write, or tell, a story about a child doing something helpful and good.

The key to opening the treasure chest is asking questions.

Chapter 5
Excellence of Learning
The Treasure Chest

1. Keys to open the treasure box are questions! What are some of your questions? What would you like to know?

    a.

    b.

    c.

2. Get someone to ask you 3 questions! And when YOU ask or answer them, you get special rewards. What are some questions and YOUR answers?

    a. Question: b. Question:

       Answer: Answer:

    c. Question:

       Answer:

3. Draw some treasures inside the treasure box. Pretend it is like your special Heart. *Fill it with things you want inside your Heart.*

Even the ants and whales pray for the teacher who teaches what is good.

Chapter 6
The Best Gift of All

If you KNOW about some good things to do, that is wonderful!

If you DO them and maybe someone else copies you, that is the BEST way to teach! What good thing will you do right now that you hope others will copy? Remember that when you DO these good things, the angels will want to be your friend and they will stroke you with their wings!!

1. Two things that you can do that you want other people to copy:

    a.

    b.

Did you know that even the whales pray for everyone, both young and old, who teach others how to be good. Put on the whales' list some good thing you have been taught by your teachers, parents and grand-parents that you can then do and others will copy.

"I get tired of playing with my toys but never tire when I am watching the beautiful animals which Allah ﷻ created, like this mother spider preparing the egg sac full of her babies."

Chapter 7
How Do You Stay Really Happy All the Time?

1. What is your favorite toy, and what is your favorite game?

    a.

    b.

2. Do you enjoy playing with these toys all day long, every single minute?

    YES __   NO __

    Do you ever get tired of playing with them?

    YES __   NO __

3. Tell about a time when you helped someone, or made someone happy, or were kind. Did you enjoy that?

4. When you do good things, they are like little doors opening for you into Paradise. Draw or Name three things you can do to open these doors into the Next wonderful World.

Now, pretend you are one of those tiny seeds you just planted!

Chapter 8
Pretend You Are A Tiny Seed

1. Find a piece of earth or a pot or dish and put earth in it. Can you get some seeds to plant? Or can you find a tiny plant to care for, to water and watch grow?

2. Now pretend *you* are the tiny plant. Isn't that fun? What do YOU need to grow? (Sun, Water, Food?) DRAW a tiny plant in the sun.

3. But you are a child, not a plant! What do you need to learn in order to grow up to be beautiful and to have a good Heart? What can you learn about that will help you go to Heaven?

    a.   b.

    c.

In the 40 books Imam al-Ghazali wrote for you, he will explain many secrets about eating, praying, and everything in your daily life that are *doors* to Paradise.

Don't most of us have too many clothes and toys? Make a list of five things that you would like to share or give away.

Chapter 9
The Three Needed Things in This Life

1. What three things do you need MOST in this world, every day?! Put a CHECK MARK beside three "MUST HAVES!":

Toys ___   A Home ___

Food ___   Games ___

Parties ___   Television ___

Clothes ___   Pets ___

2. Draw some food that is good for you on this plate.

3. Draw some clothes you like to wear.

4. Draw a few things that are in your room at home.

5. What extra clothes and toys do you have that you can give to someone in need? By doing this, you are being *generous*!!

    a.

    b.

    c.

What happens to people who spend ALL of their time busy with food, clothes or their home? What is the danger? What have they forgotten to do with their time?

6. How much of each day do you spend having fun playing? What kind of games?

1 hour ___   a.

3 hours ___   b.

6 hours ___   c.

7. How many hours do you spend doing something helpful or kind for others which pleases Allah ﷻ and makes your Heart shine?

10 minutes___

1 hours ___

2 hours ___

8. What do you do when you spend that time doing helpful things?

What are some good and kind things you can do today?

What Heart-treasure can you share?

Chapter 10
Sharing the Treasure

1. What are some of the special treasures inside your shining Heart that you can share?

Some Ideas:
Kindness
Helping Others
Sharing
Not getting angry
Not speaking badly
Doing what Mother asks you to do
Telling the truth

2. Draw jewels and write on each one some good thing you do.

How could this boy be helping his friend?

Chapter 11
What Are Things You MUST Learn?

1. What are some things that can HURT our shining Hearts?

Feeding birds ___   Being mean ___   Arguing ___
Being greedy ___   Helping Mother ___   Being grumpy ___
Being sweet ___   Sharing toys ___   Getting angry ___
Being conceited ___

2. Tell about a time when you did something that *hurt your* shining Heart.

3. Make up a story where you pretend you are very greedy and do something where you take the best for yourself.

4. What naughty ideas, that might come into your head, can you say "NO"! to? Name two:

    1. No! I will NOT_____

    2. No! _____ is not a good idea! Sorry, but I won't do that.

5. Tell a story about doing something that is giving and generous. Tell what that feels like?

6. What is the BEST answer you can give to your Mother when she asks you to do something. Maybe she asks you to pick up your toys. What do you say and then *do*?

Khadija is generous. She reads to her grandmother.

Chapter 12
Where Do They Come From,
The *Wonderful* Things We Can Learn?

1. Where do we go to find out how to have beautiful Hearts and wonderful lives?

Films ___   Parties___   Comic Books ___
The *Hadith* ___   School ___   Grandparents__
Magazines ___   Games ___   The Zoo___
The Quran ___   Friends ___   Teachers___
Television ___   Parents___   Grocery___

2. Who brought the Quran from Allah ﷻ to the Prophet Muhammad ﷺ?

   Angel's Name:

3. What kinds of things does a *hadith* tell us about our Prophet ﷺ ?

   a.

   b.

4. What are some rules we have been given from God ﷻ in the Quran, to keep our lives in good order?

   a.

   b.

   c.

What could these children be packing for their camping trip?

Chapter 13
A Family Trip
We Are on a Journey Together

1. What are some things you would need to pack for a camping trip?

   a.   b.

   c.

2. What would we need to prepare for the trip to the next Heavenly World, where we will be forever with everyone we love?

   a.   b.

   c.

3. Some ways to make our Hearts shine could be:

   a.   b.

   c.

4. What kind of people do you like most of all?

   a.   b.

   c.

5. What kind of a person are you trying very hard to BE in your life?

   a.   b.

   c.

You can't go up to the next step until you have learned everything there is to learn on the step where you are!

Chapter 14
Two Kinds of Things You Can Learn
To Make Your Heart Shine

Pretend you are on a staircase. Imagine that as you go up these steps during your life, you will one day learn the *special hidden mystical* learning. What are you learning right NOW, on the step you are on, about polishing your Heart?

Draw yourself on one of the steps. Then write one thing you learned on the step which you have now reached.

I can watch naughty thoughts and ideas, and say "NO" to them! What might this little girl be thinking about?

Chapter 15
The Story of the Pretend Two Wolves

A Useful Story we have learned from Cherokee Indians

1. Pretend you have two wolves whispering good and bad ideas to you. Draw a bad face on one and a good one on the other one! When you do what the pretend wolf is telling you to do, it's like you are feeding it and making it grow! Which wolf will you stop feeding so it will go away?

2. What could the imaginary bad wolf whisper when it wants you to do something naughty? (kinds of naughty ideas)

    a.   b.   c.

3. What does the good friendly wolf tell you that it is best to do? What kind of "food" (or ideas) makes the good wolf strong?

    a.   b.   c.

Write or tell a story about times when you feed the pretend good or bad wolves. What kind of thoughts come into your mind?

Activity Song

Make up a song with these words and add some of your own ideas:

"I Polish My Heart for Allah ﷻ"

When I help my father with the dishes,
I polish my Heart for Allah ﷻ

When I am happy for my friend who has a new toy,
I polish my Heart for Allah ﷻ

When I tell my sister, "I am sorry"
I polish my Heart for Allah ﷻ

When I am angry and take a deep calming breath
I polish my Heart for Allah ﷻ

When I _____
I polish my heart for Allah ﷻ

When I _____
I polish my heart for Allah ﷻ

When I _____
I polish my heart for Allah ﷻ

When I _____
I polish my heart for Allah ﷻ

The trust a falcon has for its master is invisible. We can see the body of this falcon with our eyes. But we understand the invisible trust of the bird and the warmth and kindness of its master with our spiritual Hearts. What we love most is invisible.

Chapter 16
Important Things You Cannot See

1. Circle what you can NOT see—that is invisible to your eyes?

A Flower   Telling The Truth   A Chair   The Sky

A Car   Kindness, Love   Your Teacher   Friendship

2. If you could only have one of these things to stay with you for the rest of your life, which would you choose to keep. Can you see it or is it invisible?

3. Describe everything that you CAN see about this falcon. What does it look like? If this falcon were yours, what invisible thing would you like most about it? Perhaps its friendship?

Chapter 17
More Ways To Make Your Heart Shine!
And the Four Imams Who Helped Us Understand What Allah ﷻ Wants Us To Do

1. Imam Shafi'i wanted the best for his friends and everyone else! Even when he was disagreeing with someone, he wanted *that* person to be right and he didn't mind being wrong.

Play this game: Pretend you are arguing with someone now. Then let that person win! Write, or tell, how that felt.

2. When Imam Malik was given gifts, he gave them away to those in need. What do you have that *you* can give away to someone who needs it?

3. Who were the other two great Imams that helped explain and organize our religion? Circle Two:

    Imam ibn Hanbal   Imam al-Bashir

    Imam Abu Bakr   Imam Abu Hanifa   Imam Hossein

4. Which kind of learning and knowledge made these four Imams so special and wise? Circle One:

    Science   Math   History   Divine Learning

    Nature Studies   Reading   Gardening   Sports

Imam Malik loved and respected learning. So when he was studying or teaching, he wanted to be at his very best so he dressed well, and sat up straight. Show how you can sit in the very best way and how to look alert. Color this.

Allah ﷻ is sending us both blessings and difficult times which are sometimes hard to understand. But God ﷻ is all-Wise and knows the reason behind everything that happens. Do YOU trust God ﷻ, who made you and the whole world, to bring you nearer to Him through the losses He has promised to every single person? All the ant is able to see is the pen and the hand, but he cannot see Who is writing.

Chapter 18
The Ant and The Pen

1. Why were the little ants sad? What turned out to be the REAL reason the zoo trip was cancelled?

2. Tell about a time when you were upset about something and then it turned out to be a good thing instead?

3. Crawl on the ground and pretend you are an ant. How high up can you see? Can you see what's happening on top of a mountain or in the tree tops?

4. Make up a story about an ant family when disappointment comes. Put Names on each of these ants.

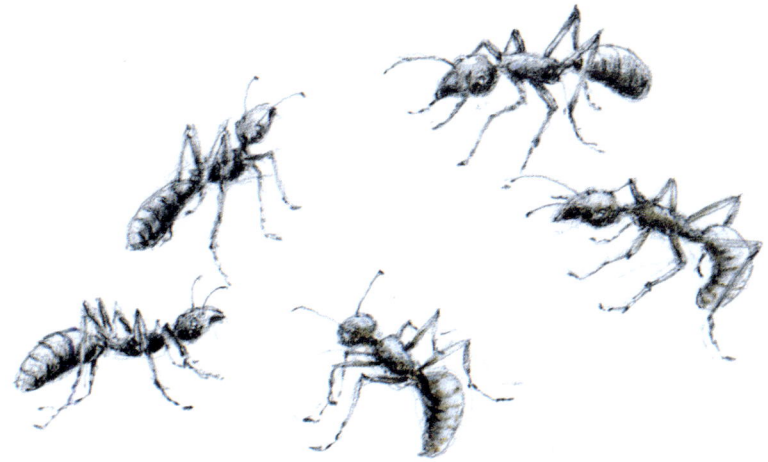

5. What did you learn from this story?

Chapter 19
The Little Boy Loses His Father's Horse

A Tale from Central Asia

1. What happened when the little boy lost his family's horse?

2. What lesson can you learn from this story?

3. Play this game: Pretend your Father comes to you with news you do not like. What are two ways you can respond?

Father says: "_____"

Your Answers—Two Kinds: The correct reply and the NOT correct reply.

a.

b.

4. The Quran says that, sometimes, something which you may think is bad for you, is really GOOD for you. Can you think of a time when this happened to you?

Imam al-Ghazali mentioned that the Prophet ﷺ said that Allah ﷻ has angels wayfaring through the sky, other than the angels that watch over humankind. When these angels see people gathering for Remembrance, they call out to one another saying, "Hasten to your Heart's desire!" Then, they surround this group and lower their wings over them, and listen!

Chapter 20
The Little Gardens Inside *The* Garden

1. If the Garden of Paradise is in the Next World, what are the "little gardens" like, that can be found in this world where we live now?

2. When people sit in a circle and say Allah's ﷻ names together, who comes to listen?

3. What can make up for 70 times of just spending your time simply playing around?

4. What are some of Allah's ﷻ names that people mention on their own or in a group? Write what each one means. Ask parents for help. Then you are "Asking a question" which is a key to the special Treasure.

What happens when a mirror gets covered with dirt or rust?

Chapter 21
How Can You Watch Your Very Own Heart?

1. If you can find a little mirror in your house, borrow it and put drops of mud all over it. Now, can you see your face correctly? Is it a true or complete image? Is that the way you REALLY look? If your Heart has dirt on it, it will not reflect things as they truly are. Draw a mirror and scribble dust and dirt all over it. Can the mirror shine very well? Can it reflect Light very well? Does it have a true, complete, and correct image of what is in front of it? Draw what a dirty heart or mirror sees.

2. What are some things you can do, when playing a game with others, that will help to polish off your dust and dots?

   a.

   b.

Every family has difficulties. Why do we say "al-hamdulilah," Praise God ﷻ, *when such trials come to us? Could it be because we are grateful to Allah* ﷻ *for giving us opportunities to purify ourselves?*

Chapter 22
Envy

The Prophet ﷺ said, "Envy devours good deeds as fire devours wood." So, we certainly don't want to ENVY someone, do we?

1. Since Envy is wanting what God ﷻ especially gave to someone else to bring that person closer to Him, why would it be silly to "envy"? Why do you prefer the life God ﷻ gave to you?

2. Do you think this family, with a child that cannot walk, "envys" people who don't seem to have any troubles?

Chapter 23
Pride and Spitefulness

1. Tell a story about a child your age who is full of pride. Do you like this person? What do they act like? Can you pretend what someone is like who thinks that he or she is better than others? Demonstrate what pride is like.

2. To be spiteful is to be mean, annoy, disappoint, and upset others. If you are unkind to someone by mistake, what is the best thing to do as soon as possible?

3. Make a story about someone at your school who acts like he or she is better than anyone else, or is "spiteful."

BRAGGING

PRIDE

BACKBITING

As a pure, little shining Heart goes up the Path of Life…

...what kinds of bad things are trying to ruin its journey?

Chapter 24
Back-Biting

1. If someone says bad things about another person when he or she is not there, why do you think this is called BACK BITING? Allah ﷻ says this is one of the worst things people do. Make up and tell a story about this. Tell what is being said and then what you would do to help, if you heard this going on?

2. Pretend you are listening to two friends talking very sweetly about someone else. What could they be saying?

3. Take some sand or grains of salt outside. Pretend these are unkind words you have said to someone. Scatter them on the ground, Try to pick them all up. They are like toothpaste squeezed out of the tube. Once out, it is too hard to get back inside. What does this game teach you? Can you draw this idea?

What is going on here? Color this drawing and think about what these children might be saying.

Chapter 25
Other Dangers! Beware of Making Excuses For Yourself, Bragging, Prying, and Spying

1. Dangers you will want to watch out for can come from *arguing*. Make up a problem and insist that *you* are the *right* one. Tell how this feels—great or not so good?

2. Pretend to brag and tell someone about something good you have done. What does it feel like. Why can something you say be called an *ugly* truth?

3. Do you keep a secret list in your mind of things people have done to you that you don't like? Why not tear up your list and forget it all and let it go? It polishes your Heart whenever you forgive. Name one thing you plan to forgive and let go.

4. Do you ever tell on your brother, sister or friend when they do something naughty? Or do you keep it to yourself, quietly? Which is *better* and *why*?

Chapter 26
Wanting The Best For Others

1. Play this game with one or two friends. Each one take turns giving good news and the others exclaim how happy they are for their friend's good news. Then do the same with sharing problems. What problem will you tell about? What would you like your friends to say or do, when you share your worry or problem? If someone wins at a game and you do not win, are you happy or unhappy? What is the best way to feel and why? How can we practice wanting the best for others?

Chapter 27
Being Two-Faced:
Hypocrisy

1. Draw a head which has two faces, one side is kind and one side is mean. Make up a story which tells how this person pretends to do something good just so *others* will *see*. Then, tell something naughty this same person also does but in *secret*.

2. Can you pronounce the word "hypocrite"? Do you ever correct your brother or sister for something you do yourself? Would it be better to do the correct thing and set an example instead? Name one thing you could do.

Chapter 28
More Problems With Arguing

1. What does God ﷻ do for people who *don't* argue and instead stay filled with peace, and are *calm and easygoing*?

2. When you hear people arguing, how does it make you feel inside? Do you want them to stop? Why?

3. Next time you are about to get into a fight over something, what *can* you do *instead*? Tell a story about this.

4. Play this game now: Get two people and let them both pretend to argue and say that they are *each* right about something. Watch it. What do you feel about it?

5. Sit quietly. Feel the goodness and light in your heart and how it fills your *whole* body. What happens now if you then get up and begin to show-off or argue?

6. Draw some stairs going up and then tell about, or write on each step, something that you do each day that takes you up higher and higher. Can you write on one step *REFUSING* TO FIGHT or argue? Write some good thing you did or said, which polishes your heart.

Chapter 29
A Question For You

1. What are you finding out from "DIVINE" Real Learning? Why do you want to do good and also, to help *others* to do well?

2. What is something you can do to help someone else?

3. What have you learned that you can do *this very moment*, which will help bring Light to your *beautiful* Heart and take you up another step? Even smiling at someone will fill his or her Heart with joy and Light. So easy to do!

4. Sometimes, we tell others to do the correct and right thing. Maybe we tell our brother or sister, "Tell the Truth! Don't Lie"! And then, in *secret*, we lie sometimes. Make up a story about someone who does this! What does this person, in your story, *say* and then what does he *do* himself that is *different*?

5. What did Iman al-Ghazali realize while he was teaching? Why did he leave teaching? What became of the Imam after he left?

6. What did al-Ghazali write while he traveled and when he came home? What did he write for us, and why? What does he want to share with us from his Real Learning?

7. What are some things that you see others doing that you really admire and like?

8. What kind of person do you want to BE? Describe:

Naughty thoughts can be like scary, barking dogs that frighten the angels away from their home in your Heart.

Chapter 30
Your Heart Is Like A House

1. In your "Heart-house" live special angels. What do they do if you get angry or envy what God ﷻ gave to somebody else instead of what He especially chose for you?

2. What could be some naughty thoughts that would seem like scary, barking dogs to your angels?

3. People build houses to live in. Allah ﷻ made your special Heart to be a place where you can find Him. What are two things you can do to make your "Heart-house" better?

    a.

    b.

This stream wasted its water and then ran out, so it couldn't make it to the Garden where it was headed. How do you spend your time? Do you save any of it for doing beautiful things?

Chapter 31
Doing Too Many Things

1. Pretend you are a stream of clear blue water, headed to bring water to a magical special garden. You have just enough water to make it there, where you will be very happy. But along the way you stop and do other things. You leave a bit of your water at the play-yard. Some at the ice-cream shop. What do you think will happen now? You no longer have enough "time" (or water) to reach The Special Garden.

2. Draw four plants below. Draw a water pitcher labeled "TIME," to water them. Time is like the water you have. You need to be careful with how you use it because you only have a certain amount. You need enough time to polish your Heart so you that can reach The Garden, shining. What amount of time do you need each day for these four activities? Write that beside each plant.

Plant 1: Sleeping and Eating

Plant 2: Learning at School

Plant 3: Games and Toys

Plant 4: Doing Good to Polish Your Heart

Chapter 32
The Teacher, The Lion, and The Jug of Water

1. If a lion gets out of its cage and someone saves you from being gobbled up, do you thank that person? What do you say?

2. If a person teaches you special "divine REAL learning" that saves you from wasting your life and makes it possible for you to go to the Garden of Paradise in the Next World, what do you say to these teachers?

3. Who are the people who teach you how to be good and nearer to God ﷻ?

    a.

    b.

    c.

4. Some people are the "know it all" type and are full of themselves. Should we be like empty, or full, glasses when we are learning? Why? How do we need to be so that wisdom and learning can be poured in?

Have you ever made a sling-shot? It takes lots of practice to hit the center of the target just like it takes lots of practice to polish your heart! What are you aiming for in your life? What is the best goal to shoot for? Why?

Chapter 33
When You Shoot An Arrow, You Need A Target

1. Draw a target with your own heart at the center. Now draw lots of arrows, or pebbles, and write on each one a way that will help you to reach the center, your shining Heart.

2. What can you practice doing every day that will make your heart better and better? A regular activity?

    a.

    b.

    c.

3. What about math and reading? Why are they important? How are they like steps on the stairway of your life? Why do you need to learn math and be able to read?:

4. Draw a heart that is like a target. Make a list of what you aim to do with your life in this world.

    a.

    b.

What would you like to name each camel?

Chapter 34
The Camels Leave

1. Draw camels in a line crossing a rocky desert. Draw people riding on their backs. What supplies do the people and camels both need for the long trip?

a. The people need_____.

b. The camels need_____.

2. What "*ideas*" do you know about which can help get you across these "rocks," or small problems which are put in your way to help you grow stronger? In what ways do these help you to grow?

a.

b.

c.

1. Now, draw **YOURSELF** with your big heart riding inside your body! What does your *heart* need for the journey through *your* life? What supplies will it need to make it *safely* across the rocky problems which *everybody* has been given in their lives, at different times?

2. What are some problems you are having at this time? How will you solve them?

   a.

   b.

   c.

What is the best REAL food you need for your heart? What small problems, like the rocks here on the path, have been sent to you so you can become stronger and better? Can you pass easily over the rocks, or the difficulties which God ﷻ kindly sends to strengthen you? Color these children pretending to be camels.

Even animal babies copy their parents who are their teachers. Name something you are copying from your parents that you love very much about them.

Chapter 35
Grandfather Explains Some Important Ideas that Seem Hard or Difficult to Understand, *At First*

1. Imam al-Ghazali tells us there are three groups of people. The people in Group ONE are busy buying things and entertaining themselves all day. Make up a story about someone like this.

2. Although the people in Group TWO live shining perfect lives, teaching all the good they learned by being good examples, most people are in Group THREE. These people learned the Special Learning and are good people from whom others can learn. But inside their Hearts is "hypocrisy" which needs a lot of polishing. Make up a story about someone in Group THREE; tell about a normal day in his or her life:

3. What group are you in?

"Grandmother, will you tell us about the THREE selves inside of us?"

Chapter 36
Grandmother Explains The Three Selves — Part 1

1. What have we been given human bodies for? Circle One.

To Play   To Meet Friends   To Watch Films

To Eat   To Get To Be Near Allah ﷻ   To Travel

To be near to Allah ﷻ, we need Special Real Learning, "divine" learning, that teaches us how to polish our Hearts exactly. God ﷻ also gives each one of us three selves to help us do this! Do you know the names of the three selves inside of you?

2. This is how it works: Each person has a low self that does things only for its own happiness! Anything naughty, and bad ideas come from this "*nafs al-ammara.*" Tell three things that your own low, false self does:

a.

b.

c.

3. But this low self is watched by another self inside you that scolds and blames the lower one. It says "You shouldn't be doing that! It's a bad idea. Stop!" The "*nafs al-lawwama*" is kept very busy trying to get the lower one to be good. Tell of 3 things you have noticed your blaming self say to your lower, false self.

a.

b.

c.

91

Describe yourself! What are you like?

Chapter 36
The Three Selves — Part 2

4. Make up two stories:

First, a story about when the low self wins and won't do what the scolding self asks but goes ahead and *does* the bad, wrong thing.

Second, make up a story about when the low naughty self *listens* to the one blaming him, and then does the *right* and correct thing:

5. But you are not either of these 2 selves. Your REAL Self, which you will experience fully when your Heart is polished clean, watches this talking back and forth. Tell of a time when you watched the low and blaming selves arguing back and forth inside your head. Maybe your mother is calling you to get up for breakfast and school. Have you noticed the lower self pretends not to hear her?

6. So, you can see how it works! The pure Heart knows what is *true*, always. The 3rd self, the *"nafs al-mutma'inna"* is at rest and peace and full joy. Don't you want to be that real, happy, good self inside of you? Well, that's where you already *are* every time you *choose* the good over the bad, and then DO the right thing. Sit quietly, shut your eyes and experience *just being* inside your shining heart. What is that like?

Chapter 36
The Three Selves — Part 3

1. Here is a head with three thought clouds above it. Write in each what the selves are thinking or saying.

Make up what the lower self might say, and how the blaming self corrects it, and include the Real You who is watching.

2. Sit quietly and watch your thoughts. Describe what they are saying. Which ones do you want to polish away? Why? Which do you want to keep? Why?

Chapter 37
Getting Rich and Getting Knowledge

1. Where can you find Real, Special Learning? Circle all the right answers:

At the store   Grandparents   At the zoo   From teachers

The Quran   In books   On television

Playing with toys   Games   Parents

Playing ball   Eating sweets   Books

2. Once you have your very Special Divine Learning which shows you how to polish your heart, what will you do with it? Circle the true answers.

     a. Keep it for yourself.

     b. Share it by being a good example yourself.

     c. Explain the good ideas to others.

     d. Not teach anything.

3. We can ALL be teachers by sharing what we have learned. By doing all the good things we learn, we are sharing! What 3 things can you do today that will show others how to behave correctly?

     a.

     b.

     c.

What is this boy teaching his little brother? How is he doing it?

Chapter 38
Being A Teacher

1. How is a teacher *supposed* to treat students? Circle what is true.

    a. Hit them if they are noisy
    b. Act as if they were his or her *own* children
    c. Be angry if the children are naughty
    d. Be sweet and loving and merciful

Since you are a teacher every moment in your life, be sure to be a good example for others.

2. What are the two best things all of the children in your class, (who are like your brothers and sisters, like your *family)*, can have together as THE goal, or target, of their *learning*?

    a. To get a good job
    b. To have people admire you and think that you are important
    c. To polish your Hearts and become shining
    d. To buy a big house
    e. To go out to eat a lot at restaurants
    f. To reach Paradise and be near God ﷻ
    g. To buy many things

3. Imam al-Ghazali has written books just for you to: (Put a check or X)

    ____ Help you know exactly how to polish the dust off your Heart
    ____ Have more time to sit around and chat
    ____ Teach you the deep meanings in life
    ____ Explain what the Prophet ﷺ brought for you from the angel Gabriel
    ____ Show you more ways to be near God ﷻ and completely happy
    ____ To win games when you play
    ____ To understand why you were born and what your life is for

Write a lesson in the teacher's book. Color the drawing and add whatever you like to decorate the classroom.

Chapter 39
Playing School:
Here is Something For *You* To Think About

1. Pretend you are the teacher. One of the children has bumped into a table of art supplies and all the paint colors have spilled and made a mess. What do you do?

   1st: Be angry at him. What would you say when you are angry?

   2nd: Make her feel she is stupid and has ruined everything? What might you say to make her feel sad?

   3rd: Tell an imaginary story about a careful, peaceful rabbit that one day was nervous and, by a mistake, knocked over and broke a vase because he was hopping too quickly. Maybe something happened at the rabbit home that has worried this poor baby rabbit. What is the best way to treat the rabbit baby that broke the vase?

2. Pretend you are a mother or father, or big brother or sister. Gently explain to your younger sisters or brothers or friends, in their own simple language, something they don't understand, or how to do something. What are gentle words you can use?

3. Are you speaking kindly and with manners? How do you treat someone with respect? Are you speaking to their low, not-real self, or are you speaking to the Real Self full of light and peace? Would that be hard to do? Try it now.

What is the best way for you to teach others?
What kind of teacher are you today?

Draw a shadow coming from each tree. Imagine their shadows are what they are teaching, being straight and good or being crooked. What kind of shadow comes from the way you are? What is your shadow like?

Chapter 40
The Two Trees

1. Draw a straight shadow coming from a straight tree. Draw straight children standing in the straight shadow copying the straight tree. People look and act like the people they copy, don't they? Put birds, leaves, fruit and flowers in the branches.

2. Draw on the shadow of a bent ugly tree, crooked people who look the same as the tree which they are copying. And then these crooked people make more crooked shadows – which are the people who then go on to copy them! Put bats on the branches and a few dead leaves.

3. Get a friend to do something silly. Then copy that person exactly. Be exactly like his or her shadow.

4. Now get someone to do a beautiful wonderful thing. Pretend you are his or her shadow. Copy that person exactly.

5. People copy each other – like being each other's shadow. What kind of things do you want others to copy that you do?

The Life of al-Ghazali

900 years ago, in a country known today as Iran

Imam Abu Hamid al-Ghazali was born in Tus, Khurasan. His family was very poor.

His father was a weaver. He died when Abu Hamid and his brother Ahmed were very young.

Before his death, he made sure his sons were put under the care of a local shaykh.

Even though this wise elder was not a scholar, he was very righteous, honorable and filled with true knowledge.

When they got older, Abu Hamid and Ahmed entered a school in Gurgan.

Imam al-Ghazali was fortunate to have one of the greatest scholars of Islam as a teacher, Imam al-Juwayni.

Ahmed eventually became a poet and a faqih. Imam al-Ghazali turned out to be one of the most intelligent and smartest people of his day. He spoke both Persian and Arabic beautifully. When he gave public lectures, people were in complete awe and amazed by the way he spoke.

At 34, he became the head of the most important and famous university in the entire Muslim world. It was called the Nizamiyyah and was in Baghdad, Iraq.

you must strive against your soul's desire ...

Day after day he would preach at people to perform great deeds.

if you do not humble yourself sincerely ...

you will never illuminate your heart

But he would grow increasingly bothered by his personality – his own arrogance, his pride and the many impurities he saw in his own heart.

How can I ask people to do good while I, myself don't practice it?

One day, Imam al-Ghazali went to class and was standing in front of the usual crowd of scholars and students.

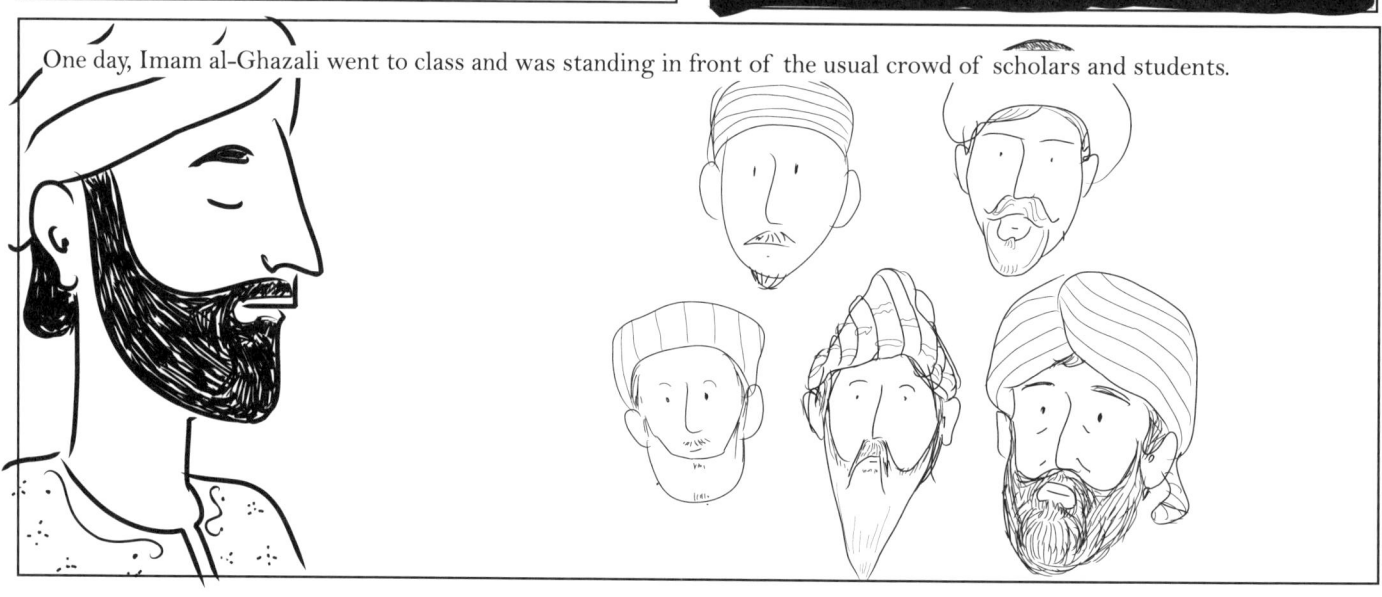

And so Imam al-Ghazali set out on his long awaited journey. He arranged everything for his wife and children and told everyone he was going on Hajj. Little did they know that his voyage would actually be his way to find the Truth, and most importantly his own true self.

He spent the next ten years of his life traveling around the Muslim world. He lived in a state of total lowliness.

The once great Imam al-Ghazali, the famous scholar and author, made a living now by sweeping the floors of the Umayyad mosque in Damascus, Syria.

His path then took him to Medina...

He prayed at the Prophet's mosque.

He performed dhikr, slowly detaching himself from this world...

Of course he visited Mecca.

There he met a group of saints.

They came from all over the world.

Together, they formed a beautiful circle of remembrance. They praised God and His Prophet all day and all night.

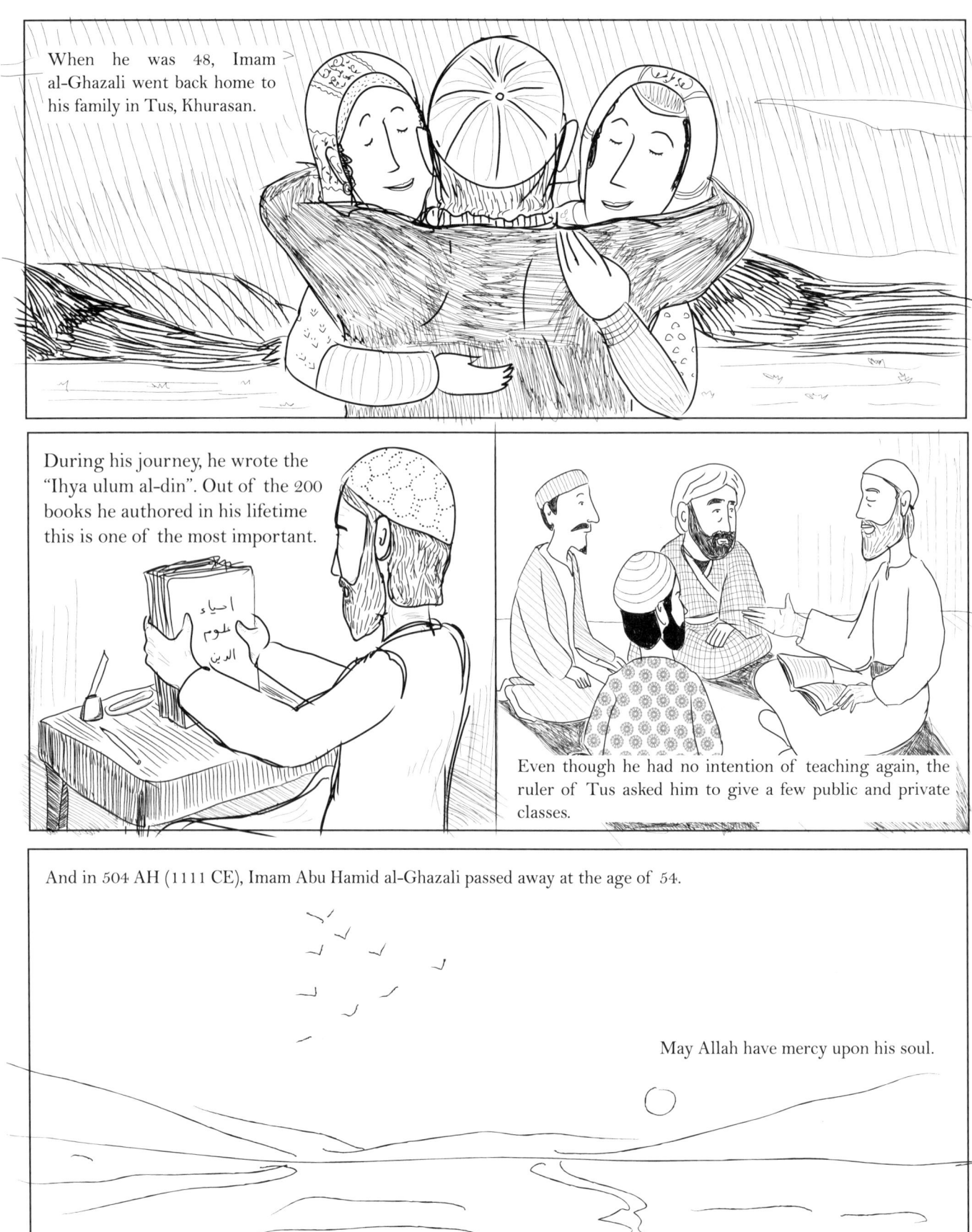

When he was 48, Imam al-Ghazali went back home to his family in Tus, Khurasan.

During his journey, he wrote the "Ihya ulum al-din". Out of the 200 books he authored in his lifetime this is one of the most important.

Even though he had no intention of teaching again, the ruler of Tus asked him to give a few public and private classes.

And in 504 AH (1111 CE), Imam Abu Hamid al-Ghazali passed away at the age of 54.

May Allah have mercy upon his soul.

You Have Two Hearts

Play this game. Each child in the group shakes a finger and says, "No!" to a naughty idea that comes to mind. Then each child tells what he or she was saying "No" to. Go around the circle playing this game three times. Color this drawing.

My Shining Heart Curriculum and Activities
A Parent-Teacher's Manual for The Book of Knowledge
Table of Contents

Fons Vitae invites parents and teachers to send us their own creative ideas for curricula and activities which will help children practice what they are learning in their daily lives. Your comments and suggestions will help Fons Vitae design future curricula and make any needed adjustments to future editions of this volume (www.ghazalichildren.org).

You will notice that several of the activities are repeated in every chapter. If a child practices or, for example, draws on his or her heart-drawing once, it will not become a conscious part of his or her life. By repeating these activities over and over again, it is hoped that the child will feel so familiar and at home with these ideas that they will become permanent habits.

A Parent-Teacher's Manual of Activities and Curriculum
To be adjusted creatively according to age groups

Message to Children, Parents, and Teachers

"God will not change the condition of a people until they change what is within themselves."
(Chapter 13, Verse 11)

Dear Children, Parents, and Teachers,

Let's change what is within ourselves for the better! That is the intention of the Ghazali Children's Series. We all feel terrible about what is going on in the world today, and we want to know what we can do about it. Allah ﷻ promises us that He will improve our situations if we improve what is inside of us, meaning our character. Our character is made up of our habits which can be good or bad actions, thoughts, or feelings. Building good character cleans our spiritual hearts and allows Allah's ﷻ beauty to shine through us. To build it, we must practice living and thinking in the best way until good habits become our way of life inwardly and outwardly. Together, we will set upon a journey to build good character and polish our hearts—helping each other along the way. Let's begin!

Teaching Methods for Parents and Teachers

Children will easily recognize and understand the truths of each teaching from Imam al-Ghazali. What is of utmost importance is that these lessons are reinforced by actually being practiced on a regular basis. In life, what we do over and over again quickly becomes a habit and the way we naturally do something. In this curriculum, we present traditional teaching methods such as review questions, crafts, and songs, but we also introduce a new method of play-learning in the spirit of prophetic instructions to let children play. Playing games and play-acting virtuous qualities is a fun and effective way for children to change their reflex reactions through repetition and allow those virtuous qualities to become second nature. For example, sharing when their first instinct is not to share—they must practice sharing in play-acting, over and over again, until it becomes easy for them and a pleasure. The success of the Ghazali Children's Series will depend upon the children being encouraged by parents and teachers in creative and enjoyable ways to practice all their learning on a regular basis.

Teacher Etiquette

- We must demonstrate to our children that we are applying the Ghazali Children's Series to ourselves and that we are willing to participate in the learning activities. For every learning activity, we strongly recommend doing exactly what the children are expected to do, yourself.

- Make the lessons in this Series a regular conversation in your family/class, and/or share the lesson plans with the families of the children in your class clearly requesting that they incorporate the Series into their family life. (Parents will be included among those referred to as "teachers" in this manual.)

- You are key to nourishing the children's motivation as you gather them to learn in a *supportive* and *non-judgmental* environment, providing positive reinforcement for their efforts.

- Have realistic expectations, based on each child's developmental level, for helping the students perform virtuous habits and putting into practice what they have been taught. Young children vary considerably in their understanding of questions and taking part in discussions.

- Be patient and encourage your student to reach his/her maximum potential and praise them often in their efforts to develop good character. Remember, you may not see all of the positive results of this Series until the children have grown into adults, but God-willing it is making a positive impact!

Program Overview

- The Ghazali Children's curriculum is a habit-forming program that builds upon itself. It includes daily, weekly, and monthly activities that are repeated in order to form good habits that enhance the inner and outer lives of children.

- After meeting on a recommended weekly basis in a formal class to learn through short and light-hearted readings, crafts, songs, and fun games, children will choose virtues from a "Secret Virtue Box," which they help to make and decorate.

- The children will perform daily practice of the virtue(s) chosen from the "Secret Virtue Box." The children will look for daily opportunities to practice their virtue(s), aiming for 40 repetitions to make it a habit.

- Alongside their "secret virtue" practice, they will use a symbolic spiritual heart craft to visualize bad habits, and plan what parts of their character they want to work on.

- As the curriculum progresses, children will begin to work in teams to donate toys and clothing to charities, cook food for those in need, and/or visit the sick/elderly. The children will work in teams to keep up at least one community service activity on a monthly basis minimum. You are essential in assisting the children in planning and arranging these repeated activities, and making sure the children keep them up. Please read ahead so that you can adequately plan for these activities.

Curriculum Specifics and Delivery

- This curriculum is intended for children ages 7 to 13 years old. The reading level of the Book of Knowledge and Book of Belief is appropriate to be read aloud by an adult to any age group. Children who are reading on grade level could read the Book of Knowledge and Book of Belief themselves if they are mid-year 3rd grade or higher. The reading materials and curriculum can be simplified for younger children as well as adjusted for older adolescents. For example, passages from the Quran and *hadith* may be more suitable for older children, while some art activities may be more engaging for the young. For curriculum updates, see www.ghazalichildren.org.

- We recommend you (the teacher) first read the chapter in the Book, the Workbook questions, and the respective activity descriptions in order to prepare class materials ahead of time.

- Always begin each lesson with *du'a'* and end with *du'a'*. We also recommend incorporating a moment of silence before you begin.

- We present various activities per chapter in order that you might choose whichever of them works best for your group of students (not because we expect you would complete all of the activities).

- The Core Lessons can serve as checkpoints for verifying that children understand the basic message of the chapters, but are not meant to be easy summaries which might diminish the process of learning through stories. The Essential Questions are meant to be open-ended and can be used during the Guided Personal Reflections and/or with older children in essay format.

- The timing and amount of material to be delivered at once is up to you, although you will notice that this curriculum is presented as if the students are meeting at least weekly. Meeting at least once weekly is recommended for the sake of habit building.

- Deliver the curriculum in the sequence presented in the Book (unless otherwise noted) because the curriculum builds upon itself. Some activities correlate to more than one chapter, and as some chapters are very short you may choose to combine chapters.

- Before moving on to a new chapter, the teacher should review the Core Lesson(s) in the previous chapter.

- During class time, the reading in the Book and the Workbook questions should precede the activities unless otherwise noted.

- You should engage the students with real life experiences and examples, give instructions, supervise discussions, and help the student when needed.

- Please create your own activities too and post them on www.ghazalichildren.org for the whole community. We simply request that you keep the activities habit-forming and fun!

- Be creative in your teaching approach and turn to Allah ﷻ first whenever inevitable challenges come up. Always feel free to reach out to Fons Vitae if you need help, and please encourage your students to frequently visit http://www.ghazalichildren.org to meet global friends and to participate in the contests associated with each book. Do submit your own insights and ideas to be shared!

Rules of Written Work

- Children may write in their Workbooks or answer Workbook questions in their own journal.

- You may photocopy pictures in the Workbook for coloring or allow children to color in their own Workbooks.

- Encourage students to keep their written work orderly and neat. Writing with a pencil instead of a pen may be neater.

- Reflection journals should be updated each time a discussion takes place.

Goals

- Teachers and students will read and discuss the text.

- Teachers and students will answer questions in the Workbook.

- Teachers and students will work together to engage in discussions regarding experiences related to the reading. Ask what each child has understood from a given chapter.

- Teachers and students will participate in in-class activities.

- Teachers and students will participate in daily-life activities.

- Teachers and students will participate in community service activities.

- Teachers and students will be role models of good character to others around them.

- Students will be more cognizant of their thoughts, actions, and words and how these relate to their spiritual hearts.

May Allah ﷻ guide each of us and our beloved children! Ameen.

General Teacher Supply List

- Adult edition as well as Children's Reader (Book of Knowledge, Book of Belief, etc.), Workbook, large item to write on such as dry erase board, large flipping paper pad on an easel, or chalkboard, corresponding writing materials.

General Student Supply List

• Reader (Book of Knowledge, Book of Belief, etc.), Workbook, composition journals (2), pencils, colored pencils, and paper for art work and drawings.

Additional Supportive Activities for Introducing the Ghazali Children's Series

Step 1: Background Story

Read the introductory story about Imam al-Ghazali and complete questions about his life with the children.

Step 2: Teacher Demonstration

Prepare a simple skit for children to watch in which adults are treating each other unkindly. For example, one adult has a delicious treat and refuses to share with the other person. Gossip, envy, hatred can also be demonstrated in short skits to the children. Tell the children that you will let them know when they can contribute to the conversation. Ask them to share what they see happening, determine if it is good behavior or not, and say what behavior would be better. Use the children's feedback to act out the skits once again. Tell the children that you will speak your negative thoughts and feelings out loud, but then stop yourself from acting upon them and instead choose the virtuous action recommended by the children.

Step 3: Making Words Clear

Children may not have a clear definition of "character," "actions," "thoughts," "feelings," and "habits." Ahead of time, create a simple definition of each and print them out on paper. Also create a board with the words and leave space to tape or paste the definition to be correctly matched by the children. Hand one definition to each child. Begin by asking the children what one word means, then ask them to find the right definition from the printed definitions. Reward the children with a treat once the correct definition is chosen. Keep the finished board visible at all times so that you and the children can refer to it as needed. Make the board large enough to add definitions as you go along like "spiritual heart," "intention," "progress," "truthfulness," "sincerity," etc.

Step 4: Discuss Pearls of Wisdom

After the children get a sense of what they will be doing with the Ghazali Children's Series, take some time to go over the following "Pearls of Wisdom" with the children and discuss why they might be important. Display the "Pearls" for future reference and/or give each child a copy to keep.

Pearls of Wisdom:

1. Become the commander of your own ship! Live by these words: "Be careful of your thoughts, for your thoughts become your words. Be careful of your words, for your words become your actions. Be careful of your actions, for your actions become your habits. Be careful of your habits, for your habits become your character. Be careful of your character, for your character becomes your destiny." —Chinese proverb

2. Focus on progress, NOT long-term goals. You will go far with Allah's ﷻ help, but it takes small steps. Measure your progress each day by checking in with yourself. Ask, "Am I making progress?" (Even a little bit counts!) Just focus on that answer being 'yes,' and don't be blinded by the long-term.

3. Cleaning one's spiritual heart is not about doing so many extra good deeds. It is about doing what we are already doing with love, kindness, and joy.

Step 5: Time Organization Tools for Children

This Series is NOT requesting that children sacrifice a lot of their playtime for extra virtuous activities. It is simply encouraging us all to do the same things we normally do in a beautiful and virtuous way. Please stress this point as a part of discussing time organization. Here are few tools you can use to talk about organizing time:

Tool 1: Check-In: Freeing Up Time for Good Deeds

Guide the children through these short questions. Repeat throughout the Series as needed.

1. Name three things that you like to do when you are not in school.

2. When do you do these activities and for how long? Which is the least important to you, and would you be willing to do something better instead?

3. Make a plan to spend less time doing one of these activities so that you have an extra 30 minutes to build good habits each day. For example, "I will spend 30 minutes less playing computer games each day so that I can help my little brother with his math homework."

4. Write notes to yourself to take 30 minutes each day to practice a new good habit, and stick them in the places that you did the old activities and on your bathroom mirror.

Tool 2: Weekly Time Tables

Assist the children to draw up simple weekly time tables that honor their need for recreation, but also promote spiritual development. They can allocate time for: 1) character building activities that beautify the spiritual heart; 2) regular school work; and 3) recreation.

Tool 3: "Planning For My Heart" Craft: Making Daily Planners

For mature children, ask them to memorize Surah al-Asr so that you can reward them with their own brand new daily planners. Provide art materials for the children to decorate the outside cover of their journals with an inspirational message about the true meaning of life. For example, Surah 2 verse 152 which reads, "Therefore remember Me, I will remember you. Give thanks to Me, and reject not Me." Covering their decorated covers with clear contact paper or tape will protect their designs.

Note for Children with Special Needs

We pray that we have all kinds of children participating in this Series including children that are ill or disabled. If a child cannot participate in some activities, please find substitutes for those children. For example, a child who is confined to their bed is in a special position to make *du'a'* for other people in need. They could also organize a charity by writing letters to donors or sharing their own story with others.

***

Chapter One Curriculum Guidance

Core Lesson: There are two kinds of learning, one practical and the other divine. Real Learning teaches us how to polish our spiritual hearts, which are different from our physical hearts. Our spiritual hearts need cleansing of vices in order to shine beautifully.

Essential Question: What is my spiritual heart and what does it need?

You may choose to read Chapter Twenty in conjunction with Chapter One during class time because Chapter Twenty narrates the characters actually creating their own "Spiritual Heart Visual Craft" (see below). It may take two sessions or a longer first session to accomplish these activities. Most of them are core activities to the curriculum so we strongly recommend completing them.

After reading and answering any questions, let the children know that you will first play a game(s) to check for understanding. Then, you will ask them to spread out in the classroom so that you can guide them through the personal reflection questions below and give them time to write and make artwork. The environment should be serene, allowing children time to focus on their feelings and relationship with God ﷻ.

New art materials, journals, or sticky notes may be laid out for the children to use for Activity 3 depending on the age group. During Activity 3, you may think about adding some soft Islamic songs to encourage the children not to speak to each other and focus on their art. Join the children in creating your own spiritual heart visual, and choose vices that you are also trying to clean away in order to set a good example for the children. Charity activities will be introduced in later chapters, but you may begin planning or participating in them now to provide ample opportunities for everyone to practice their virtues.

Activity 1: Physical Heart or Spiritual Heart?

The objective of this game is to identify which actions are connected to the physical heart and which actions are connected to the spiritual heart. The teacher will go through a list of actions and will ask the children, "Is this action connected to the physical heart or the spiritual heart?" You can use this list or come up with your own. If you would like to make this into a hands-on game, you can create paper examples of foods or activities for the physical heart and examples that are connected to the spiritual heart. Ask the children to sort them into containers listed "body/physical heart" or "spiritual heart." Hint: You can use the spiritual heart examples in "Activity 4: Spiritual Heart Visual." You will also need to create vices for Activity 4.

Examples:

Sharing—spiritual heart
Running—physical heart
Helping others—spiritual heart
When the doctor listens to your heart with a stethoscope—physical heart
Praying—spiritual heart
Feeling thankful to God ﷻ—spiritual heart
Feeling tired after exercising—physical heart
Loving others—spiritual heart
Fruit—physical heart
Vegetables—physical heart

Activity 2: The Virtues of the Messenger ﷺ Game

The purpose of this game is to introduce "virtues" to children from the example of the Prophet Muhammad ﷺ, and to emphasize core virtues of Muslims. Make sure that "virtue" has been defined on the definition board. Make a board for each child on which there is a table with three columns and three rows totaling nine blocks on a piece of paper. Randomly write the following virtues into the blocks, making the order different for each game board you create: Love, Wish good for others, Never harm anyone with words, Never harm anyone with body, Protect others from harm, Believe in Allah ﷻ with your heart and actions, Protect yourself from anger, Don't seek revenge, Forgive others.

Now share these beautiful *ahadith* with the children, and ask the children to put a treat on a virtue they learn from each *hadith*. Discuss the *ahadith* and their virtues as you play. Each *hadith* will have multiple virtues so they will quickly fill their virtue boards and can exclaim, "Al-hamdulilah!" Here are some recommended *ahadith*:

1. Anas relates that the Prophet ﷺ said: "None of you truly believes until he loves for his brother what he loves for himself," (Bukhari and Muslim). Game words: Love, Wish good for others, Believe in Allah ﷻ with your heart and actions

2. Abu Musa Al-Ash'ari, may Allah ﷺ be pleased with him, reported: I asked the Messenger of Allah ﷺ: "Who is the most excellent among the Muslims?" He said, "One from whose tongue and hands others are safe," (Bukhari and Muslim). Game words: Never harm anyone with words, Never harm anyone with body, Protect yourself from anger, Forgive, Believe in Allah ﷻ with your heart and actions, Protect others from harm

3. Narrated by Abu Hurayra, may Allah ﷺ be pleased with him: The Messenger of Allah ﷺ said, "Iman (faith) has sixty or seventy-odd branches. The least of them is to remove something harmful from the road…" (Bukhari and Muslim). Game words: Protect others from harm, Believe in Allah ﷻ with your heart and actions, Wish good for others, Love

4. On the authority of Abu Saeed Saad ibn Malik ibn Sinan al-Khudri, may Allah ﷺ be pleased with him: The Messenger of Allah ﷺ said, "Do not cause harm, nor respond to harm with harm," (Recorded in ibn Maja). Game words: Love, Never harm anyone with words, Never harm anyone with body, Protect yourself from anger, Forgive others, Don't seek revenge

Activity 3: Guided Personal Reflection

Ask the children to spread out in the classroom. Ensure a serene environment perhaps with soft Islamic songs playing in background. Verify that everyone knows what "intention" means and add it to the definition board if not already done.

Provide a coloring sheet with one of the 99 Names ﷻ written in Arabic calligraphy. When beginning the reflection, the children can color this Name ﷻ. http://freecoloringpages.co.uk/?q=99%20allah%20names

Interchange coloring with free-drawing or other forms of art in future repetitions of this activity. (Ask the children to draw something that appealed to them in the lesson and to share the meanings behind their artwork later.)

Ask the Essential Question(s) to the children, and allow them time to ponder upon their answers with their eyes closed or write it out in a personal journal. For example:

a. What is my spiritual heart and what does it need?

b. What is your intention? (Help guide the children to make their intention that of pleasing Allah ﷻ alone.)

c. Why are you trying to learn about taking care of your spiritual heart? What good things will happen to you if you take care of your spiritual heart?

Softly and kindly say something like this to the children: "Now close your eyes and focus on breathing in and out for 7 breaths repeating 'Al-' as one inhales and 'Hamdulilah' as one exhales. Try to find the deepest part inside your heart. Tell it that you wish to clean it and make it beautiful. Ask yourself everyday, 'Am I getting better?' Just focus on that answer being 'Yes.' Focus on getting better each day by sticking to good habits of thoughts, feelings, and actions. Don't worry about the far-off future just right now."

If possible, offer one-on-one time with each child to listen to their ideas and feelings about the class and daily activities, and reflect on their artwork.

Activity 4: Spiritual Heart Visual Craft

Create a visual reminder to work on improving character and polishing the spiritual heart, and keep track of improvement. It can be a journal or artwork. Here are instructions for creating a symbolic spiritual heart that can be used long-term.

Note on crafts: If you do not have the materials for a craft mentioned in this curriculum, try to find similar items that are still sturdy and attractive. Be creative.

Suggested materials:

Craft felt sheets of various colors
Construction paper of various colors
Foil
Cardboard
Journals
Scissors
Strongest glue available, with adult supervision only
Tape
Cut-outs of words or pictures of vices to be discussed in this Series. To be referred to as the "CAUTION List," it includes:

Envy, Lying, Being a Know-It-All, Arguing, Anger, Hate, Bullying, Gossip/Back-Biting, Greed, Pride, Making Excuses, Prying and Spying, Bragging/Showing Off, Being Two-Faced/Hypocrisy, Doing Too Many Things, Wasting Our Time, Ignorance, and Ingratitude (If possible, laminate the words or stick them between contact paper in order to make them durable for long-term use.)

Trace large sized hearts onto cardboard, and then re-trace onto felt sheets, foil, or construction paper. Thin artistic materials can be glued to sturdier materials for added durability. Cutting out heart shapes of materials ahead of time will make the craft easier and the product more equal from child to child. Once the spiritual hearts are designed, the children will add vices that will be discussed in the Book and Workbook.

We recommend choosing no more than four vices at a time for the children to focus on and visualize with their spiritual heart craft. (Keep the others stored away for future use.) You can use tape or another adhesive that can be removed without damaging the heart to attach the vice to the heart. You may also simply write in the words on paper hearts, but the children will need to erase and re-write in the vices several times as they go along in the Series. Younger children may be able to better understand cartoon or real picture representations of the vices better than reading the words. It also demonstrates to children the unattractive nature of these vices.

In conjunction with the next activity, "Activity 5: Secret Virtue Box," explain to the children how to use their spiritual heart visual as a tool to plan good thoughts, feelings, and actions that they will be working on.

Example of how to adjust for ages 5–7

1. Children may need one-on-one time with an adult to help write out two simple sentences. For example:
   —I promise to Allah ﷻ…
   —When I clean my heart, Allah ﷻ will make me feel…
2. Provide artwork materials beforehand for children to simply glue or paste together.

Activity 5: Secret Virtue Box

To guide the children in using their "Spiritual Heart Visual Craft," create a container with virtues written on slips of paper that the children will practice in their daily lives. The virtues that you put into the container should be the opposites of the CAUTION List words you created for the "Spiritual Heart Visual Craft." Again, we recommend putting no more than four corresponding virtues in the container at one time so that the children are not overwhelmed. Save the other virtues along with the vices you are not yet using in a safe place, and switch them out every month or whatever fits with your schedule.

Print out or write on small pieces of paper each virtue and its opposite vice from the CAUTION List. For example:

1. Envy is opposite to Wanting Good for Other People

2. Lying is opposite to Honesty

3. Being a Know-It-All is opposite to Humility and Letting Other People Be Right

4. Arguing is opposite to Calm, Respectful Discussion and Being Peaceful

5. Anger is opposite to Peacefulness

6. Hate is opposite to Love

7. Bullying is opposite to Being Friends with Everyone

8. Gossip/Back-Biting is opposite to Respecting Everyone (even when they are not around)

9. Greed is opposite to Generosity

10. Pride is opposite Humility

11. Making Excuses is opposite to Being Responsible

12. Prying and spying is opposite to Minding Your Own Business

13. Bragging/Showing Off is opposite to Modesty and Humility

14. Being Two-Faced/Hypocrisy is opposite to Integrity/Truthfulness

15. Doing Too Many Things is opposite to Concentrating on What's Important

16. Wasting Our Time is opposite to Making Good Use of Your Time

17. Ignorance is opposite to Seeking Knowledge

18. Ingratitude is opposite to Gratitude and Patience

19. Meanness is opposite to Kindness

Add these slips to a special container that you can refer to as the "Secret Virtue Box." Each child will randomly choose two slips of paper and whatever virtues they have chosen will be their special virtues to practice for the next two weeks. Because of the number of virtues to cover, we recommend that the children choose two virtues at a time. If you have more time or want to simplify it, just choose one virtue at a time. Return the slip of paper to the container after the children write in their journal which virtues they will practice for the next two weeks.

The goal is to practice each virtue at least 40 times in order to help it become a habit, but counting forty times may be too cumbersome for the children. So while you may mention the "40 times makes a habit" rule to the children, simplify it for them by just asking the children to look for opportunities to practice the good deed in their daily-life activities. The children can record a few instances per day in which they practiced the virtue in a personal journal or planner, or if they cannot yet write discuss in class.

As this activity is ongoing throughout the curriculum, having the children pick new virtues bi-weekly will allow the in-between weeks for reflection time with the repeated activity "Guided Personal Reflection and Update Spiritual Heart Visual" (in upcoming chapters). Make sure to share this part of the curriculum with parents so that they can support their child in practicing the virtue/refusing vices.

Activity 6: Jennah's List of Ways to Polish the Heart

Read the following "Ways to Polish the Heart" to the children to give them ideas for practice (submitted by an 11-year old girl to Fons Vitae). Assist the children in relating each good deed to a virtue you put into the Secret Virtue Box.

"Jennah's List of Ways to Polish the Heart"

Try one of these each day and notice how lovely it feels:

1. When my parents ask me to do something difficult, like chores, I will not complain. Rather I will try my best to do whatever they ask of me.

2. If someone bothers me, or says unkind things to me, I will control my temper.

3. Whenever I do something, like make my bed or fold clothes, I will try to do it beautifully and neatly.

4. I will spend the day with my grandparents to make them happy.

5. After a snowstorm, I will shovel my neighbor's driveway before they wake up.

6. I will be the first to say sorry when my friend and I have an argument. (Or be the first to greet the other person cheerfully upon seeing him/her again.)

7. I will read the story of the Prophet Muhammad ﷺ every year.

8. I will smile more often.

9. I will place a birdbath in the yard for birds who need a drink of water.

10. I will always say "Bismillah" before starting anything.

11. I will write to my grandparents who live far away. I want them to feel happiness when they see a letter in their mailbox.

12. I will keep a nice book or magazine on the kitchen table for my Dad to read in the morning as he eats breakfast.

13. I will help put away the groceries.

14. I will keep extra change in the car, so that my mom can quickly hand money to someone in need while we are driving someplace.

15. I will empty the dishwasher every morning.

Chapter Two Curriculum Guidance

Core Lesson: Animals are different from people because human beings have spiritual hearts. There are two kinds of nourishment: one for the bodily heart and one for the spiritual heart.

Essential Question: What makes me special among Allah's ﷻ creation?

The goal of this chapter is for children to understand their special status in Allah's ﷻ creation, and therefore that their purpose in life and responsibility *is* to become good human beings. They should understand that they are different than animals because they have a spiritual heart, and building good character is what makes their spiritual heart pure.

Please also remind the children about the Pearls of Wisdom activity. Emphasize again to just focus on "getting better" everyday so that the children do not feel overwhelmed. Ask the children to take turns reading each point aloud.

Activity 1: Connecting to the Quran

Read to the children from Surah 2 verse 197:

"O our Lord give us some good in this world and in the next abode" and reflect upon Hasan al-Basri's commentary: "Verily in this world it is knowledge and worship; in the Next Abode, the Garden." How is this different from the needs of animals?

Activity 2: A Moment of Silence

Have the children write down this formula for seeking knowledge, then repeat it back to you and discuss it: "Knowledge begins with silence, then hearing, then memorizing, then performance, and then spreading it."

The one that is often forgotten is silence. After reciting the beginning *du'a'*, this is an excellent way to begin every class. Ask the children to close their eyes if necessary and just focus on breathing in and out peacefully.

Activity 3: Animal Observation

Make a trip to the park, animal farm, or zoo and ask the children to watch the way the animals behave in general and around meal time. If not possible, show them a video of animals in a group who are presented with food. Ask the children, "How do the animals behave?" and "What do they do with their time all day?" Use a Venn diagram, photograph, or another visual method to aid your discussion.

Activity 4: Role play

Among the children and adults, choose who will be animals and who will be the human who feeds the animals. Provide craft materials for the children to create animal masks (optional). Split the children into groups if the class size is too large. Place pretend food or real treats in the middle and ask the children to pretend to be just like the animals at mealtime. Once the children begin to pretend like they are not sharing, ask them to now demonstrate the way human beings should behave.

Make the point that this activity is not just about learning how ridiculous it looks not to share, but about the children realizing that, because they are human, they have the ability to learn how to behave in the most beautiful way. Most of the children already know that it is best to share. That's great. Now there are other manners and good habits that must be learned—that is what this Series is about. This is the special knowledge made just for humans because we have spiritual hearts.

Activity 5: Sing Dawud Wharnsby's "I'm Just a Rock"

This is a delightful song with a catchy tune about accepting the position Allah ﷻ gave each of us and its duties and privileges. Children love it. Here's the link: https://www.youtube.com/watch?v=wOfrz96knv8

"I'm Just a Rock"

I'm just a rock
and everyday I sit and watch the sky.
I sleep here in the sun and rain
and do not question why.
I don't want to be a bird
cause us rocks were never meant to fly.
But you can sit and rest on me
When you pass by.

Al-hamdulilah, al-hamdulilah, I'm a rock

And that is all Allah asks of me.
Al-hamdulilah, al-hamdulilah, I'm a Muslim
And there's nothing else I'd rather be.

I'm just a tree
And this is the only life I'll ever know.
I bow my boughs in worship
Whenever I feel the wind blow.
And my purpose in life
Is to grow when Allah says grow
And be a home for the birds and shade
For folks below.

Al-hamdulilah, al-hamdulilah, I'm a tree
And that is all Allah asks of me.
Al-hamdulilah, al-hamdulilah, I'm a Muslim
And there's nothing else I'd rather be.

I'm just a person
And my life is full of opportunity.
I can travel through the world
Over land and over sea.
But will I choose the path of Truth
Or a path to misguide me?
Sometimes I wish I had a simple life
Just like a rock or a tree.

But al-hamdulilah, al-hamdulilah, I'm a person,
and Allah has given me a choice that's free.
So, al-hamdulilah, I choose to be a Muslim
And there's nothing else I'd rather be.

Activity 6: Guided Personal Reflection and Update Spiritual Heart Visual

This activity corresponds to the Secret Virtue Box and is ideally used as a reminder to the children after the first week of practicing their secret virtue (to be repeated each time a new virtue is chosen).

Ask the children to spread out in the classroom with their Spiritual Heart Visual craft and/or journals. Ensure a serene environment perhaps with soft Islamic songs playing in background. Verify that everyone knows what "intention" means and add it to the definition board if not already done.

Provide a coloring sheet with one of the 99 Names ﷻ written in Arabic calligraphy. When beginning the reflection, the children can color this Name ﷻ. http://freecoloringpages.co.uk/?q=99%20allah%20names

Interchange coloring with free-drawing or other forms of art in future repetitions of this activity. (Ask the children to draw something that appealed to them in the lesson and to share the meanings behind their artwork later.)

Suggested Script:

1. Ask the Essential Question(s) of the chapter to the children, and allow them time to ponder upon their answers with their eyes closed or write it out in a personal journal.

2. Softly and kindly say something like this to the children: "Now close your eyes and focus on breathing in and out for 7 breaths repeating 'Al-' as one inhales and 'Hamdulilah' as one exhales. Try to find the deepest part inside your heart. Tell it that you wish to clean it and make it beautiful. Ask yourself everyday, 'Am I getting better?' Just focus on that answer being 'Yes.' Focus on getting better each day by sticking to good habits of thoughts, feelings, and actions. Don't worry about the far-off future just right now."

3. "Open your eyes and update your Spiritual Heart Visual removing any vices that you have avoided and keeping any vices that you are still trying to improve. Do not despair if vices remain—your intention is what matters!"

4. "Write down what you would like to improve and name at least one easy way that you can improve."

5. If possible, offer one-on-one time with each child to listen to their ideas and feelings about the class and daily activities, and reflect on their artwork.

Chapter Three Curriculum Guidance

Core Lesson: There are two worlds—this brief life that is filled with suffering and loss, and the next life, which is perfect and forever. Real Knowledge is directly from Allah ﷻ to us (which came through his Archangel Jibril to the Prophet Muhammad ﷺ). Real Knowledge teaches us how to prepare for the next world where we will meet our Most Compassionate Lord ﷻ and to live beautiful lives now.

Essential Question: Has Allah ﷻ sent me Real Knowledge and, if so, why did He do this?

Meet these lessons with amazement as children need motivation to do the hard work of improving their habits and building good character. The purpose of the suggested activities is to strengthen their desire for knowing God ﷻ and being in Paradise.

Activity 1: Connecting to the Quran

Read to the children Surah 9 verse 72, and reflect upon its meaning in relation to the necessity of strengthening one's spiritual heart:

"Allah has promised to believers—men and women—Gardens under which rivers flow, to dwell therein (forever), and beautiful mansions in Gardens of everlasting bliss. But the greatest bliss is the Good Pleasure of Allah. That is the supreme joy (or success)."

Activity 2: Allah ﷻ Speaks to Me

As in every activity, be as creative as possible to bring the beauty of Islam into the children's artwork. Preparing attractive and sturdy resources ahead of time will help children produce beautiful work they will be proud of and that will last throughout the duration of this Series.

Create a visual for the children to see the chain of transmission from Allah ﷻ to the Archangel Jibril to the Prophet Muhammad ﷺ to the child. It can be a wall hanging, a page in their journals, the cover of a folder they will be using in this Series, a bookmark, etc. The point is that they will see this representation of the chain of transmission and remember this special connection to God through receiving His knowledge. At www.freeislamiccalligraphy.com you can download free printouts of beautiful Islamic calligraphy with Allah's ﷻ name or the name of His Beloved ﷺ. Or you can make calligraphy yourself or use decorative English words. You may print out pictures of the children ahead of time to represent the child's position at the bottom of the chain of transmission or simply write out his/her name.

Activity 3: The Islamic *Isnad* Tradition

Inviting a guest speaker to a classroom or home school environment can be very refreshing. In this case, look for an individual in your community who has been granted permission through an *isnad* chain to teach Quran or other Islamic teachings. Ask the speakers to tell their personal stories to the children, which illustrate how knowledge is passed down. While the goal is to emphasize to the children that they are each recipients of religious knowledge, it will hopefully be inspiring to the children to know that they could become fine people or even scholars of special status who teach others.

Activity 4: Dreaming about Heaven—It's better than you can imagine!

May be used with Chapter Three or Chapter Four

The purpose of this activity is to create internal motivation for purifying one's heart, and to help make rewards in the afterlife more meaningful. Depending on the age of the children, and their ability to write, lead an activity asking the children to imagine heaven and think about all the things they would want. Suggested activities include writing a page in their journal, making artwork by drawing, painting, or cutting out beautiful photos for a collage, or simply sitting with another classmate and sharing their dreams of heaven. Remember to tell the children that as wonderful of a place they can imagine that heaven will be, Allah ﷻ says it will be even better than that with things in store that we could have never dreamed of! And most important, the pleasure of being near to Allah ﷻ! Share this *hadith qudsi* with the children: "I have prepared for My servants what no eye has seen, no ear has heard and no human heart can imagine."

Activity 5: Secret Virtue Box

After allowing the children some time (recommended two weeks if possible) to practice their virtue, offer the Secret Virtue Box to each child so that a new virtue may be chosen, read, and noted, and then the slip of paper returned to the container. Remind the children of the Pearls of Wisdom, and talk positively to them about their efforts so far. You may choose to provide healthy treats around this time to make it pleasurable.

Chapter Four Curriculum Guidance

Core Lesson: The sinking of a boat is like a person when he or she dies. The only thing that doesn't sink and that remains with you is Real Knowledge and a purified spiritual heart.

Essential Question: What are the most important belongings that I can carry with me always?

With the children's morale high, this is a good time to initiate community service activities to be repeated throughout this Series and God-willing throughout their lives.

Please also remind the children about the Pearls of Wisdom and emphasize again to just focus on "getting better" everyday. Ask the children to take turns reading each point aloud.

Activity 1: Toy Boat Craft

Suggested materials:

Cardboard shoe boxes, juice boxes, plastic container, or any other sturdy household item that can serve as a toy boat structure. This website has several different ideas: http://kidsactivitiesblog.com/56539/boat-crafts-kids-make
Washable non-toxic paint, wrapping paper, or appropriate art materials to decorate the boat
Construction paper of various colors for the sail
A stick for the sail
Strong glue, with adult supervision only
Tape

The toy boat craft will be used in this chapter as well as Chapter Eleven in the "I am the Commander of My Ship" craft in which students will add a paper doll of themselves to the toy boat. Hence, construct this boat with that activity in mind. Find sturdy materials and art supplies that the children can use to make toy boats. Ask them to imagine packing all their toys into the boat (maybe add some paper toys inside), and then setting out to sea when a storm comes in and tips over the boat. They lose all their material belongings, but thanks be to God ﷻ, they survive.

Now they take a second journey by boat, but this time they pack only what will benefit them in case the boat sinks and they don't get another chance to live. Discuss the quote, "Someone said to one of the wise men (*hukama*), "What things do you acquire?" He replied, "Those things which will float with you when your boat sinks; that is knowledge." One said, "By the sinking of the ship, he meant the destruction of his body by death."

Activity 2: The Belongings of Paradise Charity Box

Remind the children that, "While we do not bring any belongings from this life into Heaven, that's all right because the more good deeds we do in this life, Allah ﷻ will give us even better gifts and everlasting happiness in this world and in Paradise."

Going along with the Workbook questions, introduce giving charity as a good deed that will yield happiness right now and Paradise later on. Ask the children to bring in an attractive toy and/or article of clothing that is in good condition to be put in a group charity box for a local orphanage, homeless shelter, or community center for the poor. The children can decorate the box as a group craft to give them a sense of ownership. Emphasize to the children that the reward of charity is for giving away things that they would like to use, but they are willing to give it up for somebody else to enjoy. Also, Allah ﷻ knows how rich or poor each of us are, and He ﷻ asks that we each give our fair portion only. As long as what we give is a fair portion of our wealth, He ﷻ will reward the same no matter if it is big charity or small charity.

Schedule a day to bring in donations and remind the parents and children. Repeat this activity bi-weekly or monthly, and have the children take turns delivering the items to a chosen charity organization. We recommend that the children bring in only one item at a time so that they will have items to give in the future.

Activity 3: Make a "Good Habit Calendar"

With the children, use a large sheet of paper or another material that you can write on to make a calendar of the current month and the month ahead. Keep this calendar displayed in your meeting area. Schedule in days for collecting items for the group charity box, and the day that it will be distributed and by which child. Other group charity ideas will be introduced in the following chapters and you will need time and space to schedule those as well.

Activity 4: Guided Personal Reflection and Update Spiritual Heart Visual

Ask the children to spread out in the classroom with their Spiritual Heart Visual craft and/or journals. Ensure a serene environment perhaps with soft Islamic songs playing in background.

Provide a coloring sheet with one of the 99 Names ﷻ written in Arabic calligraphy. When beginning the reflection, the children can color this Name ﷻ. http://freecoloringpages.co.uk/?q=99%20allah%20names

Interchange coloring with free-drawing or other forms of art in future repetitions of this activity. (Ask the children to draw something that appealed to them in the lesson and to share the meanings behind their artwork later.)

Suggested Script:

1. Ask the Essential Question(s) of the chapter to the children, and allow them time to ponder upon their answers with their eyes closed or write it out in a personal journal or draw a picture which relates to it.

2. Softly and kindly say something like this to the children: "Now close your eyes and focus on breathing in and out for 7 breaths repeating 'Al-' as one inhales and 'Hamdulilah' as one exhales. Try to find the deepest part inside your heart. Tell it that you wish to clean it and make it beautiful. Ask yourself everyday, 'Am I getting better?' Just focus on that answer being 'Yes.' Focus on getting better each day by sticking to good habits of thoughts, feelings, and actions. Don't worry about the far-off future just right now."

3. "Open your eyes and update your Spiritual Heart Visual removing any vices that you have avoided and keeping any vices that you are still trying to improve. Do not despair if vices remain—your intention is what matters!"

4. "Write down what you would like to improve and name at least one easy way that you can improve."

5. If possible, offer one-on-one time with each child to listen to their ideas and feelings about the class and daily activities, and reflect on their artwork.

Chapter Five and Chapter Six Curriculum Guidance

Core Lessons: A way to open the heart is by asking questions and then teaching what you learn to others by example. The angels, the ants and the fish in the sea ask God ﷻ to bless those who teach by example—by practicing what they have learned.

Essential Questions: How can I open my spiritual heart for Real Knowledge? How do I make sure that I have really learned something? Why do the angels, ants, and fish in the sea ask God ﷻ to bless the one who teaches by example? How can I be included in this miracle?

Emphasize to the children that teaching is done not just through speaking, but more importantly through our actions! Point out to the children that as they have been practicing virtuous habits, they have been teaching other people about good character. Teaching others good habits pleases Allah ﷻ and He rewards us.

Activity 1: Connecting to the Quran

Read with the children and reflect upon Surah 38 part of verse 9:

"Say: "Can they who know and they who do not know be deemed equal?"

Activity 2: Opening a Treasure Chest

Share the following *hadith* with the children: "Knowledge is a treasure chest, the keys of which are the asking of questions. Therefore ask, for truly four persons are rewarded by it, namely; the one who asks, the one who is learned, the one who hears, and the one who loves them." Assign the children investigative work to do before the next meeting. Each child should seek out a parent, a teacher, or a learned Muslim elder to ask a question they are curious about. They might need your help developing their questions. The children should write down the answer and then present it to the other students and teacher at the next meeting.

Activity 3: We All Teach Game

This game involves each child taking turns to mention a lesson that he/she has learned from another child. It is better if the lesson is an action instead of something the person has said. Once someone has mentioned a lesson then it is the next person's turn until everyone has had a turn. If you are in a class with students who do not know each other well, each student could share something learned from a family member. Be sensitive if a child has lost a parent. Accept any answer, unless it is disrespectful, as you are building a relationship of trust with the children.

For example:

Mom: "Daddy always says Bismillah before eating, so now I know to say it too."

144

Then it is the next child's turn:

Child #1: Daddy always says please and thank you, so now I know to say it too."

Then it is the next child's turn:

Child #2: Daddy always shares food with people who come to our house, so now I know to share too."

Next switch to things that mother teaches and so on.

Activity 4: Teach Like the Beloved Messenger of God ﷺ

Break up the students into teams and have one student pretend he/she is giving advice to another student, but being harsh in tone, impolite, and rude. Now announce that the Prophet Muhammad ﷺ was the opposite of this. Ask them to role play the way the Prophet Muhammad ﷺ would have taught others by smiling, using soft language, speaking to people according to their level of understanding, and being gentle in his approach. Guide the children to discuss *adab* and add it to the definition board. What is the importance of *adab* (polite manners)? If we have good *adab*, others will learn from us but when we present ourselves with bad *adab,* this may be copied by others.

Activity 5: Secret Virtue Box

After allowing the children some time (recommended two weeks if possible) to practice their virtue, offer the Secret Virtue Box to each child so that a new virtue may be chosen, read, and noted, and then the slip of paper returned to the container. Remind the children of the Pearls of Wisdom, and talk positively to them about their efforts so far. You may choose to provide healthy treats around this time to make it pleasurable.

Chapter Seven Curriculum Guidance

Core Lesson: There are two kinds of happiness: temporal and eternal.

Essential Question: Where does the deep feeling of happiness come from and how can I get it?

Activity 1: Connecting to the Quran

Read to the children Surah 29 verse 64, and reflect upon its meaning:

"What is the life of this world but amusement and play? But verily the Home in the Hereafter, that is life indeed, if they but knew."

You might ask the children to think about a time they have been deeply happy and to describe that. Then ask the child about a time when he or she was happy and then suddenly sad.

Activity 2: Smile Please!

Describe to the children the beautiful smile of the Prophet Muhammad ﷺ! To put everyone in a light mood, have the children pair off for "smile contests"—whoever can smile the longest at another person wins a healthy treat. (Hint: Let everyone win a treat in the end so that the children's spirits remain high.)

Or play "pass the smile" where everyone sits in a circle, and the first person smiles with the biggest smile they can to the person on their right and so on passing smiles all around. Emphasize making a habit of always smiling when greeting their teachers, parents, friend, siblings,…everyone. Even if one is not feeling well, it is important to greet everyone with a respectful tone of voice.

The Prophet Muhammad ﷺ said "Even meeting your brother with a cheerful face is charity."

Activity 3: The Belongings of Paradise Charity Box

Schedule this day on your calendar so that the children are prepared and have chosen an item to bring into the classroom for the charity box. Remind the children something like, "While we do not bring any belongings from this life into Heaven, that's all right because the more good deeds we do in this life, Allah ﷻ will give us even better gifts and everlasting happiness in this world and Paradise."

Before the children put their donations into the box, ask them to remember using the item and how happy they felt at the time. Then ask them to explain why they don't use the item anymore. After they answer, explain to them again that these toys only bring happiness for a short period of time, but the actions that strengthen the spiritual heart will bring happiness in this world and the next.

Repeat this activity bi-weekly or monthly, and have the children take turns delivering the items to a chosen charity organization. We recommend that the children bring in only one item at a time so that they will have items to give in the future.

Activity 4: Guided Personal Reflection and Update Spiritual Heart Visual

Ask the children to spread out in the classroom with their Spiritual Heart Visual craft and/or journals. Ensure a serene environment perhaps with soft Islamic songs playing in background.

Provide a coloring sheet with one of the 99 Names ﷻ written in Arabic calligraphy. When beginning the reflection, the children can color this Name ﷻ. http://freecoloringpages.co.uk/?q=99%20allah%20names

Interchange coloring with free-drawing or other forms of art in future repetitions of this activity. (Ask the children to draw something that appealed to them in the lesson and to share the meanings behind their artwork later.)

Suggested Script:

1. Ask the Essential Question(s) of the chapter to the children, and allow them time to ponder upon their answers with their eyes closed or write it out in a personal journal.

2. Softly and kindly say something like this to the children: "Now close your eyes and focus on breathing in and out for 7 breaths repeating 'Al-' as one inhales and 'Hamdulilah' as one exhales. Try to find the deepest part inside your heart. Tell it that you wish to clean it and make it beautiful. Ask yourself everyday, 'Am I getting better?' Just focus on that answer being 'Yes.' Focus on getting better each day by sticking to good habits of thoughts, feelings, and actions. Don't worry about the far-off future just right now."

3. "Open your eyes and update your Spiritual Heart Visual removing any vices that you have avoided and keeping any vices that you are still trying to improve. Do not despair if vices remain—your intention is what matters!"

4. "Write down what you would like to improve and name at least one easy way that you can improve."

5. If possible, offer one-on-one time with each child to listen to their ideas and feelings about the class and daily activities, and reflect on their artwork.

Chapter Eight and Chapter Nine Curriculum Guidance

Core Lesson for Chapter Eight: This world is like a seedbed giving us time and a chance to grow into our true selves.

Essential Questions for Chapter Eight: How do I want to grow? Who do I want to become?

Core Lesson for Chapter Nine: Some people waste so much money and time going beyond their three worldly needs—food, clothing and shelter—that they waste their opportunity to focus on their spiritual heart and growing into their best self.

Essential Questions for Chapter Nine: Do too many material belongings ever distract me from doing good deeds? How can I stop it?

Activity 1: Connecting to the Quran

Read and try to paraphrase Surah 5 verses 87–88 to the children, and ask them to reflect together on its meaning:

"O ye who believe! make not unlawful the good things which Allah hath made lawful for you, but commit no excess: for Allah loveth not those given to excess. Eat of the things which Allah hath provided for you, lawful and good; but fear Allah, in Whom ye believe."

Activity 2: Watch "The Story of Stuff"

This is a fun 20-minute documentary that does a superb job of educating about material surplus in an inspirational manner. Children tend to enjoy it and easily understand its message: https://www.youtube.com/watch?v=9GorqroigqM

Activity 3: Plant a Seedling

Talking about the needs of plants and human beings alongside the needs of the spiritual heart helps children to understand that they must care for their spiritual hearts. Use the Workbook questions to make sure the children understand the three needs of plants: 1. Nutritious soil, 2. Water, and 3. Sunlight and the three physical needs of human beings: 1. Shelter, 2. Food, and 3. Clothes. Guide the children to also understand three needs of the spiritual heart: 1. Authentic knowledge of Allah ﷻ, 2. Prayer to and remembrance of Allah ﷻ, and 3. Good deeds for the sake of Allah ﷻ alone. You could post a list of these needs somewhere in your classroom and have the students copy them down in their journal or incorporate them into the decoration of the seedling pot.

Suggested supplies:

Plastic cups or small planting pots
Sand or fine gravel
Rye grass seeds or marigold seeds, or whatever seeds are readily available to you (ideally something fast growing)
Potting soil
Scissors
Art materials to decorate cups such as paints, decorative tape, construction paper, wrapping paper, stickers, and glitter glue
Pictures of the children (optional) to decorate the pots so that the growing grass becomes like hair (which can even be trimmed with scissors as a game)

Put sand or gravel in the bottom of a plastic cup or small pot for drainage and add potting soil to within an inch of the top of the container. Sprinkle rye grass seeds thickly on top of the soil or follow the instructions on the package of whatever seed you choose. Keep the seeds moist with water but do not soak. Place the pots in a location that receives ample sunlight. Marigold and rye grass seeds grow very quickly—about three to five days.

If your children are using a personal planner, help remind them to practice their secret virtue by incorporating four empty check boxes for each day into the planner. After each day, ask the children to check the first box if they watered the pot to help the seed grow, check the second box if they did something to care for their physical body, check the third box if they did something good to help their spiritual heart grow (praying, sharing, being nice to others), and the fourth box if they had time to play.

It is useful to discuss how much time was spent on each activity, and use the "Check-in: Freeing Up Time for Good Deeds" activity to help achieve balance. Remember the fourth box is important, as there is prophetic instruction that parents give children time for good recreation. Please also be a part of this activity so you can set an example for the children on how to manage time. Show them how much time you spend on your own spiritual heart.

Activity 4: Sing Dawud Wharnsby's "Rose"

A beautiful song about growing into the best human being possible:

https://www.youtube.com/watch?v=E_2fcd3g0y4

"Rose"

I wonder if a thorny twig even knows,
that one day it will blossom and will grow a lovely rose.

I wonder of my own life, what is it I'll be?
The twiggy little stick I am—will I become a tree?

Roots so deep and strong, my arms up to the sky?
Bring cool shade, sweet fruits and flowers to those who pass me by?

God gives us choices to grow in better ways.
Our best is yet to come, as long as we wake to new days.

So, though today I'm small, there will come an hour.
Tomorrow may be my day, to blossom, bloom and flower.
If it's meant to be, and God wills it for me,
I will beautify this world, like a rose bush or fruit tree.

Just be patient with me, we'll wait and see.

Activity 5: Secret Virtue Box

After allowing the children some time (recommended two weeks if possible) to practice their virtue, offer the Secret Virtue Box to each child so that a new virtue may be chosen, read, and noted, and then the slip of paper returned to the container. Remind the children of the Pearls of Wisdom, and talk positively to them about their efforts so far. You may choose to provide healthy treats around this time to make it pleasurable.

Chapter Ten Curriculum Guidance

Core Lessons: It is important to share the jewels of the spiritual heart. The brain can know *about* God ﷻ, but the spiritual heart can come to know Him ﷻ in a special way. The God-given essence of a child (*dhat al-tifl*) inclines him or her towards faith and understanding what is possible or impossible.

Essential Questions: What kind of special jewels are in my own spiritual heart?

Activity 1: Connecting to *Hadith*

Read this *hadith* to your children and reflect upon its meaning, ideally in conjunction with the next activity, "My Bright and Shining Heart": "There lies within the body a piece of flesh. If it is sound, the whole body is sound; and if it is corrupted, the whole body is corrupted. Verily this piece is the heart," (Bukhari and Muslim).

Activity 2: My Bright and Shining Heart

This activity is only appropriate for mature children with adequate adult supervision. Small flashlights can also be used as "pretend candles." Gather the children in a circle in a room that you can make dark. Everyone will hold one candle. Turn off the lights and tell the children that this is what it is like when your spiritual heart is not being taken care of. Then light your candle. After your candle is lit, mention to the children that, even though the flame is small, it provides enough light for everyone to see each other. This flame represents a spiritual heart of a virtuous person that has good deeds. Then using your flame, light the candles of each child. Tell them that the strong spiritual heart, like the flame, is able to give to others without losing any of its light.

Activity 3: "To Know Someone" Game

The purpose of this game is to show the children that more is gained and understood by being in a teacher's presence than by merely hearing a description later of what was taught. Try to find two different guest speakers (ideal) or videos of well-liked respected elders or scholars that the majority of the children have never seen or met before. If coming to your class, ask the guests to have a special message to give to the children. If not possible to have guests, Celebrate Mercy has a collection of videos from luminous scholars sharing a short message about the Prophet Muhammad ﷺ. Their videos would be ideal: https://www.youtube.com/user/CelebrateMercy

Break up the children into two groups. Group A will get to meet the first guest and listen to his/her short message while Group B is not present. The speaker will then leave or the video will be turned off, and Group B will come back into the room without having heard the speaker. Group A will try to explain who they met and what they learned to Group B. Emphasize to the children to take note of how they felt while being in these groups. Now repeat and exchange roles. Ask the children questions along these lines:

1. How did it feel to be the one who was present before the speaker versus being the one who only got to hear about him/her later?

2. Which group did you prefer to be in?

3. Why was it easier to learn or understand from being there first-hand?

Gently make the point that the difference in satisfaction is even greater for someone who has a polished heart and can know Allah ﷻ because of it, and someone whose heart is dark and cold. The second can listen to religious knowledge and benefit, but they do not experience the wonderful joy of knowing Allah ﷻ in their heart. Praise the children for polishing their hearts and tell them how proud you are of them for trying hard and not giving up.

Activity 4: Sing Zain Bhika's "The Heart of a Muslim"

Here is the link: https://www.youtube.com/watch?v=s70rcys_LjA

"The Heart of a Muslim"

Looking up at the sky, searching for Allah Most High
He rejected the way of worshipping gods of clay
The Prophet Ibrahim knew that Allah was near
And that the heart of a Muslim is sincere

Under the hot burning sun, he declared God is one
Though with stones on his chest, his *iman* would not rest
The Muezzin knew that right would conquer wrong
And the heart of a Muslim must be strong

Chorus:

149

It's the heart of a Muslim through the guidance of Islam
That makes you fair and kind and helpful to your fellow man
So living as a Muslim means that you must play a part
Allah looks not at how you look, but what is in your heart

In our poor meager state, little food on our plate
Mother said she was glad, always sharing what we had
When I asked how can we share what's not enough
She said the heart of a Muslim's filled with love

He said it's time you should know, you will learn as you grow
That some people around will do what's bad to bring you down
Father said to be a star that's shining bright
For the heart of a Muslim does what's right

Chorus

So whatever you do, make sure your words are true
Honesty is the best, because life is a test
Even if it hurts so much you want to cry
For the heart of a Muslim does not lie

Chorus

Activity 5: Guided Personal Reflection and Update Spiritual Heart Visual

Ask the children to spread out in the classroom with their Spiritual Heart Visual craft and/or journals. Ensure a serene environment perhaps with soft Islamic songs playing in background.

Provide a coloring sheet with one of the 99 Names ﷻ written in Arabic calligraphy. When beginning the reflection, the children can color this Name ﷻ. http://freecoloringpages.co.uk/?q=99%20allah%20names

Interchange coloring with free-drawing or other forms of art in future repetitions of this activity. (Ask the children to draw something that appealed to them in the lesson and to share the meanings behind their artwork later.)

Suggested Script:

1. Ask the Essential Question(s) of the chapter to the children, and allow them time to ponder upon their answers with their eyes closed or write it out in a personal journal.

2. Softly and kindly say something like this to the children: "Now close your eyes and focus on breathing in and out for 7 breaths repeating 'Al-' as one inhales and 'Hamdulilah' as one exhales. Try to find the deepest part inside your heart. Tell it that you wish to clean it and make it beautiful. Ask yourself everyday, 'Am I getting better?' Just focus on that answer being 'Yes.' Focus on getting better each day by sticking to good habits of thoughts, feelings, and actions. Don't worry about the far-off future just right now."

3. "Open your eyes and update your Spiritual Heart Visual removing any vices that you have avoided and keeping any vices that you are still trying to improve. Do not despair if vices remain—your intention is what matters!"

4. "Write down what you would like to improve and name at least one easy way that you can improve."

5. If possible, offer one-on-one time with each child to listen to their ideas and feelings about the class and daily activities, and reflect on their artwork.

Chapter Eleven Curriculum Guidance

Core Lessons: Before children are old enough to perform all the pillars of faith, they can do good and guard against such harm as greed, conceit, showing off, self-centeredness and learn to watch and correct thoughts as they arise.

Essential Question: What does it mean to be in control of myself? Do I want to be in control of myself?

Activity 1: Connecting to the Quran

Read Surah 26 verses 87–89 to the children, and reflect on its meaning:

"And let me not be in disgrace on the Day when we will be raised up, the Day when neither wealth nor children will be of use, but only the one who brings to God a sound heart." Inform the children that this was the prayer of the Prophet Ibrahim, peace be upon him.

Activity 2: Act It Out! Game

Ask the children to think of real-life scenarios which represent the following vices and virtues, and then turn these scenarios into skits to demonstrate to the rest of the class. As a transition from the vice skit to the virtue skit, have the actor say aloud to the group a command to his ego, such as, "No, I will not be greedy! I will share!" Here are three vices/virtues to act out:

1. Greed versus charity
2. Bad intentions/ideas versus good intentions/ideas
3. Arrogance versus humility/modesty

You can also involve yourself in acting out the vices and virtues. For example, set up a scenario in which you have a toy and your child asks if he or she can play with the toy. Then tell your child that you are going to act very selfishly and not share the toy. After you act it out, ask your child what he or she thought about it. How did he or she feel? Then act it out again but this time share the toy. Before you share the toy make sure you say out loud something like "I don't want to share this toy. Wait, this is a bad thought. I do not want to act on bad thoughts. I am going to share this toy to make everyone happy!"

Point out to the child that each of us has the power to command ourselves. Act out the same two scenarios again but this time reverse the roles, and have the same discussions after each scenario. Make sure to ask your child how it felt to do a bad deed, how it felt to do the right thing, and how it feels to be in control of yourself.

Activity 3: "I am the Commander of My Ship" Craft

This fun craft allows the children to make themselves the commander of the toy boats which they constructed earlier in the Series. Ask the children to think about what it means to be the commander of one's ship as they are doing the craft. Find instructions in Chapter Four's Activity 1.

Instruct the children to use the art materials to create miniature paper dolls of themselves to glue to the mast of the sail. It is optional to add their photos. Make the point that to command one's ship means to take charge of our thoughts, feelings, and actions-steering them in a positive direction.

Activity 4: Family Coupons of My Shining Heart

In conjunction with the virtue chosen from the Secret Virtue Box or as a separate activity, provide construction paper and writing utensils to the children in order to design coupons for their family. These coupons can be used whenever their family member needs their help. Communicate this with the family members so that they use the coupons within the next two weeks. For example, "I will wash the dishes" or "I will call Grandma two times this week to see how she is doing."

Activity 5: The Belongings of Paradise Charity Box

Schedule this day on your calendar so that the children are prepared and have chosen an item to bring into the classroom for the charity box. Remind the children something like, "While we do not bring any belongings from this life into Heaven, that's all right because the more good deeds we do in this life, Allah ﷻ will give us even better gifts and everlasting happiness in this world and Paradise."

Before the children put their donations into the box, ask them to remember using the item and how happy they felt at the time. Then ask them to explain why they don't use the item anymore. After they answer, explain to them again that these toys only bring happiness for a short period of time, but the actions that strengthen the spiritual heart will bring happiness in this world and the next.

Repeat this activity bi-weekly or monthly, and have the children take turns delivering the items to a chosen charity organization. We recommend that the children bring in only one item at a time so that they will have items to give in the future.

Activity 6: Secret Virtue Box

After allowing the children some time (recommended two weeks if possible) to practice their virtue, offer the Secret Virtue Box to each child so that a new virtue may be chosen, read, and noted, and then the slip of paper returned to the container. Remind the children of the Pearls of Wisdom, and talk positively to them about their efforts so far. You may choose to provide healthy treats around this time to make it pleasurable.

Chapter Twelve Curriculum Guidance

Core Lesson: We can trust what we are asked to do because it comes directly from God ﷻ through his Angel and the Prophet ﷺ, from Quran and *Hadith*.

Essential Questions: What role does the Prophet Muhammad ﷺ play in my life? How can I increase my love for him ﷺ?

Activity 1: Connecting to the Quran

Read to the children verse 107 from Surah 21 and reflect on it together:

"And we have not sent you [O Muhammad] except as a mercy to the worlds."

Activity 2: Thank You O Messenger of Allah ﷺ

Gather the children in a circle with their "Allah ﷻ Speaks to Me Craft" from Chapter Three. Present each child with a copy of their own Quran and tell them, "Allah ﷻ sent down the Quran to the Prophet Muhammad ﷺ through the Archangel Jibril in small parts. Over the span of 23 years, the Archangel Jibril gave the Prophet Muhammad ﷺ parts of the Quran. The Quran that we have today is the collection of all the parts that the Archangel Jibril came to give to the Prophet ﷺ, and it has been preserved for over 1000 years word for word just so you and I can learn it exactly as it was revealed. Not a single word has changed. As you learn about the second half of the shahada, you will come to know and love the Prophet Muhammad ﷺ who sacrificed his life and that of his family to make sure you would have Allah's ﷻ words in your hands today. Knowing this makes us love him, and by practicing his beautiful habits we experience firsthand how his *sunna* brings happiness into one's life."

Ask the children to go around in the circle and name one thing they are thankful for from the Prophet Muhammad ﷺ.

Activity 3: Smile Please!

No matter what acts of charity the group partakes in, remind the children to stay positive, put others before themselves, and TRY TO KEEP SMILING just like the beautiful smile of the Prophet ﷺ! To put everyone in a light mood, have the children pair off for "smile contests"—whoever can smile the longest at another person wins a treat. (Hint: Let everyone win a treat in the end so that the children's spirits remain high.) Provide options to help the children handle any difficult feelings that come up such as one-on-one time with an adult mentor, quiet time, or ability to change activities.

Or play "pass the smile" where everyone sits in a circle, and the first person smiles his or her biggest smile to the person on the right and so on passing smiles all around. Emphasize making a habit of always smiling when greeting their teachers, parents, friend, siblings…everyone.

The Prophet ﷺ said, "Even meeting your brother with a cheerful face is charity."

Activity 4: The Message Movie

Reward the children's efforts and inspire them by watching "The Message" film or Sira cartoon. Here they are for free:

http://www.dailymotion.com/video/x2ewzp3_the-message-full-movie-in-english_shortfilms

http://youtu.be/vGxVWDLO87I

Activity 5: Serve Like the Prophet Muhammad ﷺ!

Choose a community project to complete every month. Here are two ideas which can adjusted according to circumstance:

1. Feed Your Neighbor: Contact a local homeless shelter or orphanage and ask about their policy for bringing food to the residents. Then allow the children to plan a meal that they will drop off to the homeless shelter that same week. Find a location where the children can cook together. Small teams will allow each child to feel like he/she has an important role.

2. Visit the Sick and Elderly: Contact a nursing home for the elderly and ask about its policy for visitation. Allow the children to pick a time and activity that they would like to do with the residents. Encourage the children to be excited about visiting the elderly and reinforce how much the residents will appreciate it. However, please have a serious discussion with the children ahead of time about expectations for visiting the elderly including showing them the utmost respect and always being kind no matter what. Discuss with the children that they might see people who are very ill physically or mentally. The children should not speak loudly and should ask any questions to the teacher in the group, not the residents.

Activity 6: Making the Habit

Share with the children the following *hadith*: Aisha said that Rasul Allah ﷺ said: "The deeds most loved by Allah ﷻ (are those) done regularly, even if they are small," (Bukhari and Muslim). After the children have participated in both charities, have a class discussion on making a monthly commitment to at least one charity. Now is the time to use the "Good Habit Calendar" that you may have made earlier in the Series. Assign each child or team a task to commit to in order to make it a team effort. Encourage the children to keep up both charities if desired or split up and rotate. Assigning groups may help everyone feel included.

Activity 7: Guided Personal Reflection and Update Spiritual Heart Visual

Ask the children to spread out in the classroom with their Spiritual Heart Visual craft and/or journals. Ensure a serene environment perhaps with soft Islamic songs playing in background.

Provide a coloring sheet with one of the 99 Names ﷻ written in Arabic calligraphy. When beginning the reflection, the children can color this Name ﷻ. http://freecoloringpages.co.uk/?q=99%20allah%20names

Interchange coloring with free-drawing or other forms of art in future repetitions of this activity. (Ask the children to draw something that appealed to them in the lesson and to share the meanings behind their artwork later.)

Suggested Script:

1. Ask the Essential Question(s) of the chapter to the children, and allow them time to ponder upon their answers with their eyes closed or write it out in a personal journal.

2. Softly and kindly say something like this to the children: "Now close your eyes and focus on breathing in and out for 7 breaths repeating 'Al-' as one inhales and 'Hamdulilah' as one exhales. Try to find the deepest part inside your heart. Tell it that you wish to clean it and make it beautiful. Ask yourself everyday, 'Am I getting better?' Just focus on that answer being 'Yes.' Focus on getting better each day by sticking to good habits of thoughts, feelings, and actions. Don't worry about the far-off future just right now."

3. "Open your eyes and update your Spiritual Heart Visual removing any vices that you have avoided and keeping any vices that you are still trying to improve. Do not despair if vices remain—your intention is what matters!"

4. "Write down what you would like to improve and name at least one easy way that you can improve."

5. If possible, offer one-on-one time with each child to listen to their ideas and feelings about the class and daily activities, and reflect on their artwork.

Chapter Thirteen Curriculum Guidance

Core Lessons: Life's journey must include polishing one's heart in order to enter the Next World. Life's focus cannot be entirely on getting things. We, and our very lives, "look like" what we are striving to get.

Essential Questions: What am I striving for in my life? What do I want to strive for?

Activity 1: Connecting to the Quran

Read to the children verse 39 from Surah 53 and reflect upon its meaning:

"Man does not receive other than that for which he strives."

Hint: Define "strive" on the definition board!

Activity 2: Witness God's Beautiful Creation

Make the theme of Chapter Thirteen come alive and refresh the children's spirits by taking them on a field trip to a natural beautiful scenery. You can complete the chapter reading and/or Quran reflection as the children sit in a circle. Provide delicious food. If you can, build a campfire, eat delicious treats and sing the beautiful songs you have been learning about Allah ﷻ and His prophets, peace be upon them all.

Activity 3: The Journey of My Life Walk

Along with Activity 2 above or separately, invite the children to go on a silent walk with you. The purpose of staying silent is so that the children can think about a very important question: "What do I want to strive for in my life?" On the first part of the walk, tell the children to list for themselves freely everything that they want to strive for without any judgement about what is best. Inform the children that at one point in the walk everyone will make a right turn, and at that point they should decide what is the absolute most important and best thing to strive for in their lives. You can give them examples before the walk begins of things that can be sought from the readings or from your own ideas. You will alert them

154

when to make the "right turn."

End the walk in some place scenic where the group can stand in a circle and voluntarily share what they discovered about their life goals. God-willing everyone will answer with a virtuous idea of what they want to strive for in their lives. If one child does not give a virtuous answer, be careful not to shame the child by pointing it out in front of everyone. Instead, give that child extra attention and love later on and check for understanding from the previous readings and activities.

Activity 3: Sing Silent Sunrise by Dawud Wharnsby and Yusuf Islam

Here is a beautiful song which speaks to the mission of the Ghazali Children's Series. Perfect for children to sing along with the below lyrics. Here is the link:

https://www.youtube.com/watch?v=AIRbDQ0byV8

"Silent Sunlight"

La ilaha illa-Allah
La ilaha illa-Allah

Silent sunlight welcome in, There is work I must now begin
All my dreams have blown away
And the children wait to play, They'll soon remember things to do
When the heart is young and the night is done and the sky is blue

La ilaha illa-Allah
La ilaha illa-Allah

Morning song birds sing away
Lend a tune to another day
Bring your wings and choose a roof
Sing a song of love and truth

We'll soon remember if you do
When all things were tall
And our friends were small
And the world was new

La ilaha illa-Allah
La ilaha illa-Allah

Sleepy horses heave away
Put your backs to the golden hay
Don't ever look behind at the work you've done
For your work has just begun

There'll be the evening in the end
But till that time arrives
You can rest your eyes
And begin again

La ilaha illa-Allah
Silent sunlight
La ilaha illa-Allah
Morning sun
La ilaha illa-Allah
Silent sunlight welcome in

Activity 4: Secret Virtue Box

After allowing the children some time (recommended two weeks if possible) to practice their virtue, offer the Secret Virtue Box to each child so that a new virtue may be chosen, read, and noted, and then the slip of paper returned to the container. Remind the children of the Pearls of Wisdom, and talk positively to them about their efforts so far. You may choose to provide healthy treats around this time to make it pleasurable.

Chapter Fourteen Curriculum Guidance

Core Lesson: There are two kinds of the Real Divine Learning. The highest is reached by slowly and carefully ascending each step, learning everything one can while on that step.

Essential Questions: What have I learned in the past about my relationship with God ﷻ? What am I currently learning on the steps I am on?

Activity 1: Connecting to the Quran

Read Surah 71 verses 13–14 to the children, and reflect upon its meaning:

"What's wrong with you that you don't place your hope in God's Beneficence, seeing that it is He Who has created you in successive stages."

Activity 2: Baking into My Best Self

For this activity, you will need to find a simple recipe. It does not need to be baking as the title of the activity suggests, but children do tend to enjoy baking. Along with the children, follow the instructions of the recipe. After you have completed the recipe, ask the children to think back to the reading and think about what things made the recipe a success? Wait until the children answer that following the instructions and going from one step to the next in order is what made the baking successful.

Remind them that this is similar to polishing their hearts in that one must complete the first step properly before moving on to the next one. Also, just like baking in a hot stove changes ingredients into something better, the difficult steps we take in life can also make us into something wonderful.

Activity 3: My Life Book

In this craft, the children will learn a surprising truth about their lives: that everything they feel, think, and do can be recorded in their "Life Book." Just like a famous author writes an amazing story that the reader loves to read, each of us is also trying to write an amazingly beautiful life story in our "Life Book." Provide the children with folded together pieces of card stock paper, construction paper, blank stationary, or a blank children's books (which can be bought at craft stores or online). They may also use a page in their journal. The children will write the life story they would want Allah ﷻ to read about them. Depending on the age of the children, they may need one-on-one assistance to write in a story-like format. Illustrations are welcome.

The following is an example: Maryam Nur was born on January 10th, 2004, to her mother and father. As a little girl she loved to…As she grew up she learned to…"help the poor by making food for them"… "always tell the truth"…Sometimes Maryam struggled because…"it was hard to share"…"other children teased her and she became upset"…but she learned to overcome this by…"loving to make other people happy"…"forgiving other people." When she grew up she became a…"scholar of Islam"…"doctor"… "fireman"… She helped everyone around her by…She was known to be…"kind," "helpful," "humble." She lived her life in service of Allah ﷻ.

Activity 4: Children's Poem to accompany "My Life Book"

Incorporate poetry into your classroom by simply reading a poem to the children, writing it out beautifully on the cover of their "My Life Book" craft, or even having them memorize it. Shaykh Abdal Hakim Murad has published a fantastic children's book with classical Islamic poetry for children entitled *Montmorency's Book of Rhymes*. An example is (from p. 93 of the book):

"In Allah's ﷻ great Book, where but angels look
On pages of spotless beauty,
Are written in letters of living light
A Muslim's life and his duty"

Activity 5: Guided Personal Reflection and Update Spiritual Heart Visual

Ask the children to spread out in the classroom with their Spiritual Heart Visual craft and/or journals. Ensure a serene environment perhaps with soft Islamic songs playing in background.

Provide a coloring sheet with one of the 99 Names ﷻ written in Arabic calligraphy. When beginning the reflection, the children can color this Name ﷻ. http://freecoloringpages.co.uk/?q=99%20allah%20names

Interchange coloring with free-drawing or other forms of art in future repetitions of this activity. (Ask the children to draw something that appealed to them in the lesson and to share the meanings behind their artwork later.)

Suggested Script:

1. Ask the Essential Question(s) of the chapter to the children, and allow them time to ponder upon their answers with their eyes closed or write it out in a personal journal.

2. Softly and kindly say something like this to the children: "Now close your eyes and focus on breathing in and out for 7 breaths repeating 'Al-' as one inhales and 'Hamdulilah' as one exhales. Try to find the deepest part inside your heart. Tell it that you wish to clean it and make it beautiful. Ask yourself everyday, 'Am I getting better?' Just focus on that answer being 'Yes.' Focus on getting better each day by sticking to good habits of thoughts, feelings, and actions. Don't worry about the far-off future just right now."

3. "Open your eyes and update your Spiritual Heart Visual removing any vices that you have avoided and keeping any vices that you are still trying to improve. Do not despair if vices remain—your intention is what matters!"

4. "Write down what you would like to improve and name at least one easy way that you can improve."

5. If possible, offer one-on-one time with each child to listen to their ideas and feelings about the class and daily activities, and reflect on their artwork.

Chapter Fifteen Curriculum Guidance

Core Lesson: In order to teach about awareness, self-observation and self-correction, an imaginary story about two wolves is helpful. One is naughty, the other is good. If one listens to what the naughty wolf suggests, it is like feeding him. If one ignores this wolf, it starves and goes away. The good wolf is nourished and remains.

Essential Question: How can I make my "good wolf" as strong as can be? How can I starve my "bad wolf"?

Activity 1: Connecting to the Quran

Read to your children Surah 114, and reflect upon its meaning:

Say, "I seek refuge with the Sustainer of humankind, the Sovereign of humankind, the God of humankind, from the mischief of the slinking whisperer who whispers in the hearts of human beings among jinn and among humankind."

Activity 2: Two Wolves Game

Suggested supplies:

Two shoe boxes, baby wipe containers, or any other container that you can decorate to make it look like a wolf

Art materials such as construction paper, paint, wrapping paper, cotton balls to decorate the boxes into wolves

Beforehand or with the children, make one box into an attractive "good wolf," and one box into an ugly "bad wolf." Cut out a hole for the mouth of the wolf or use the opening of the baby wipe container. Write down examples of deeds that are both good and bad on small cards of the same size that can fit into the mouths of the "wolves."

Collect all the cards and begin to play the game. Each child gets to pick a card and determine which card is food for which wolf. If each child makes their own wolves, they can also use this craft as a way to examine their own character. If the child follows through on a good thought or action, tell them to feed the good wolf. If they are about to do something bad or want to do something bad, warn them about feeding the bad wolf. If they follow through on a bad thought or action, then tell them to feed the bad wolf. If they do not do it, congratulate them because that counts as a good deed! Feed the good wolf instead.

Activity 3: *Nur* is a *Sunna*

Reward the children with a treat or small gift for memorizing, in English or Arabic, a special *du'a'* for *nur* (light) to enter their hearts. They can recite it daily and especially while prostrating in prayer just like the Prophet Muhammad ﷺ!

You can find it here: http://authentic-dua.com/2011/12/10/duaa-of-light-noor/

Allaahummaj'al fee qalbee nuran, wa fee lisaanee nuran, wa fee sam'ee nuran, wa fee basaree nuran, wa min fawqee nuran, wa min tahtee nuran, wa 'an yameenee nuran, wa 'an shimaalee nuran, wa min 'amaamee nuran, wa min khalfee nuran, waj'al fee nafsee nuran, wa 'a'dhim lee nuran, wa 'adhdhim lee nuran. Waj'al lee nuran, waj'alnee nuran. Allaahumma 'a'tinee nuran, waj'al fee 'asabee nuran, wa fee lahmee nuran, wa fee damee nuran, wa fee sha'ree nuran, wa fee basharee nuran (Bukhari and Muslim).

O Allah ﷻ, place light in my heart, and on my tongue light, and in my ears light and in my sight light, and above me light, and below me light, and to my right light, and to my left light, and before me light and behind me light. Place in my soul light. Magnify for me light, and amplify for me light. Make for me light, and make me light. O Allah ﷻ, grant me light, and place light in my nerves, and in my body light and in my blood light and in my hair light and in my skin light (Bukhari and Muslim).

Activity 4: *Reminder* The Belongings of Paradise Charity Box

Schedule this day on your calendar so that the children are prepared and have chosen an item to bring into the classroom for the charity box. Remind the children something like, "While we do not bring any belongings from this life into Heaven, that's all right because the more good deeds we do in this life, Allah

ﷻ will give us even better gifts and everlasting happiness in this world and Paradise."

Repeat this activity bi-weekly or monthly, and have the children take turns delivering the items to a chosen charity organization. We recommend that the children bring in only one item at a time so that they will have items to give in the future.

Activity 5: Secret Virtue Box

After allowing the children some time (recommended two weeks if possible) to practice their virtue, offer the Secret Virtue Box to each child so that a new virtue may be chosen, read, and noted, and then the slip of paper returned to the container. Remind the children of the Pearls of Wisdom, and talk positively to them about their efforts so far. You may choose to provide healthy treats around this time to make it pleasurable.

Chapter Sixteen Curriculum Guidance

Core Lesson: Things that are invisible such as kindness and friendship are more precious to us than what we can see with our eyes, and can never be taken away from us.

Essential Questions: Which is more important to me—the material or the invisible? How do I engage with the important invisible things in my life? Give one example.

Activity 1: Connecting to the Quran

Read to the children Surah 2 verses 1–4, and reflect upon the importance of believing in the unseen:

"Alif Lam Mim. This is the Book; in it is guidance sure, without doubt, to those who fear Allah. Who believe in the Unseen, are steadfast in prayer, and spend out of what We have provided for them. And who believe in the Revelation sent to thee, and sent before thy time, and (in their hearts) have the assurance of the Hereafter. They are on (true guidance), from their Lord and it is these who will prosper.

You can review the six "unseen" articles of faith in Islam with the children, and perhaps let them earn a small prize for memorizing them.

1. Belief in God ﷻ
2. Belief in the Angels
3. Belief in Divine Books
4. Belief in the Prophets
5. Belief in the Day of Judgment
6. Belief in God's ﷻ predestination

Activity 2: Invisible to Us, but Loved So Much: the Prophet Muhammad ﷺ

This is an incredibly beautiful short film about a young French boy who is asked to draw the Prophet Muhammad ﷺ. His response is breathtaking and it teaches us about how to love and recognize Rasul Allah ﷺ in our own lives, and also how to respond to negativity with something better. Here is the link: http://themuslimvibe.com/videos/from-the-web/a-muslim-student-is-asked-to-draw-prophet-muhammad-his-response-is-breathtakingly-beautiful-video/

Activity 3: "Do You Believe in the Unseen?" Game

The purpose of this activity is to help the children realize that belief in the unseen makes sense, and also to point out how much we value things that are not material. This game is better if the two partners are family members or close friends, but it can work with fellow students as well.

Have the children break up into groups of two. First, tell the children to smile, say something nice, and give their partner a big sincere hug. Ask, "Could you feel that person's care and/or love for you?"

Next have one child blindfold the other child so that they cannot see anything. Again, tell the children to smile, say something nice, and give their partner a big sincere hug. Exchange blindfolds, and repeat. Ask the children, "Could you feel that person's care and/or love for you this time? Did it matter if you could see them or not—did you still know that they loved you?" Guide the children to recognize that many very important things, like "love," are unseen but we know in our hearts that they truly exist.

Activity 4: Random Acts of Kindness

Ask the children if they know what a "random act of kindness" is? Ask for the children to share real-life examples and write them on the board. Point out how random acts of kindness spread invisible feelings of peace and joy to everyone as they are often contagious—once you help someone randomly they feel the need to do the same for someone else! Assign the children to be leaders in initiating a chain of random acts of kindness. At the next meeting time, the children can share their experience with the class.

Activity 5: The Belongings of Paradise Charity Box

Schedule this day on your calendar so that the children are prepared and have chosen an item to bring into the classroom for the charity box. Remind the children something like, "While we do not bring any belongings from this life into Heaven, that's all right because the more good deeds we do in this life, Allah ﷻ will give us even better gifts and everlasting happiness in this world and Paradise."

Before the children put their donations into the box, ask them to remember using the item and how happy they felt at the time. Then ask them to explain why they don't use the item anymore. After they answer, explain to them again that these toys only bring happiness for a short period of time, but the actions that strengthen the spiritual heart will bring happiness in this world and the next.

Repeat this activity bi-weekly or monthly, and have the children take turns delivering the items to a chosen charity organization. We recommend that the children bring in only one item at a time so that they will have items to give in the future.

Activity 6: Guided Personal Reflection and Update Spiritual Heart Visual

Ask the children to spread out in the classroom with their Spiritual Heart Visual craft and/or journals. Ensure a serene environment perhaps with soft Islamic songs playing in background.

Provide a coloring sheet with one of the 99 Names ﷻ written in Arabic calligraphy. When beginning the reflection, the children can color this Name ﷻ. http://freecoloringpages.co.uk/?q=99%20allah%20names

Interchange coloring with free-drawing or other forms of art in future repetitions of this activity. (Ask the children to draw something that appealed to them in the lesson and to share the meanings behind their artwork later.)

Suggested Script:

1. Ask the Essential Question(s) of the chapter to the children, and allow them time to ponder upon their answers with their eyes closed or write it out in a personal journal.

2. Softly and kindly say something like this to the children: "Now close your eyes and focus on breathing in and out for 7 breaths repeating 'Al-' as one inhales and 'Hamdulilah' as one exhales. Try to find the deepest part inside your heart. Tell it that you wish to clean it and make it beautiful. Ask yourself everyday, 'Am I getting better?' Just focus on that answer being 'Yes.' Focus on getting better each day by sticking to good habits of thoughts, feelings, and actions. Don't worry about the far-off future just right now."

3. "Open your eyes and update your Spiritual Heart Visual removing any vices that you have avoided and keeping any vices that you are still trying to improve. Do not despair if vices re-

160

main—your intention is what matters!"

4. "Write down what you would like to improve and name at least one easy way that you can improve."

5. If possible, offer one-on-one time with each child to listen to their ideas and feelings about the class and daily activities, and reflect on their artwork.

Chapter Seventeen Curriculum Guidance

Core Lesson: Imam al-Ghazali shares details with us about the exemplary quality of the inner lives and practice of the four great Imams—their humility, generosity, honesty, worldly poverty, night prayer vigils and purity.

Essential Question: What was one thing you particularly liked about the Imams' lives? Why?

Activity 1: Connecting to the Quran

Read Surah 58 verse 22 to the children, and reflect upon its meaning in relationship to those special people who have attained Divine Learning:

"(Those who believe in God and the Last Day,) it is they in whose hearts He has inscribed faith, and whom He has strengthened with inspiration from Himself and whom He will admit into gardens through which running waters flow, therein to abide. Well-pleased is God with them, and well-pleased are they with Him. They are God's people: oh, truly, it is they, the people of God, who shall attain to a happy state!"

Activity 2: The Four Imams Activity

Follow the Chapter Seventeen Workbook activities. While the children are playing the pretend arguing game, ask them to learn and repeat Imam Shafi'i's *du'a'* for his opponent. You can write it on the board so that they can refer to it during their game, and copy it into their journal:

" O Lord, help him so that truth may manifest itself in his heart and on his tongue. If it be that the truth is on my side, may he follow me; and if the truth be on his side, may I follow him."

Activity 3: Secret Virtue Box Special Edition

Let the children know that this week you will be adding special virtues from the first two Great Imams to the Secret Virtue Box. Have the children choose from these virtues only this week and then add them back to the general collection in the coming weeks: "Keeping your good deeds a secret like Imam Shafi'i," "Letting other people win the argument and saying *du'a'* for them like Imam Shafi'i," "Giving away perfectly good gifts to others like Imam Malik," "Keeping good posture and dressing beautifully for learning like Imam Malik." Remind the children that it is all right to let their parents know about their good deeds as they might need their help.

Activity 4: *Reminder* Serve Like the Prophet Muhammad ﷺ

Smile please! This is a friendly reminder to keep up the group charity projects scheduled on your Good Habit Calendar such as feeding the poor or visiting the elderly/sick. Remind the children to stay positive, put others before themselves, and TRY TO KEEP SMILING just like the beautiful smile of the Prophet Muhammad ﷺ! To put everyone in a light mood, have the children pair off for "smile contests"—whoever can smile the longest at another person wins a treat. (Hint: Let everyone win a treat in the end.) Provide options to help the children handle any difficult feelings that come up such as one-on-one time with an adult mentor, quiet time, or ability to change activities.

Remember that Aisha said that Rasul Allah ﷺ said: "The deeds most loved by Allah (are those) done regularly, even if they are small," (Bukhari and Muslim). Also keep in mind that the children might need to have regular check-ins about how their service projects are going. That's normal, things are bound to come up! Help them smooth out any difficulties.

Chapter Eighteen Curriculum Guidance

Core Lesson: Imam al-Ghazali's story about the ant is a metaphor for the importance of trusting God ﷻ always, knowing that both easy and difficult times come from His loving plan for our spiritual well-being.

Essential Question: What is the best way to be if unwelcome news comes?

Activity 1: Connecting to the Quran

Read to the children from Surah 2 part of verse 216:

"But it may well be that you hate a thing the while it is good for you, and it may well be that you love a thing the while it is bad for you: and God knows, whereas you do not know."

Activity 2: How Wolves Change Rivers Short Film

This is a glorious true story about how an apparent hardship turned into a major blessing. Since we have also used bad wolves as a metaphor, you may need to clarify for the children that now we are looking at how something originally thought to be hardship (the wolves) turned into a blessing. Here is the video: https://vimeo.com/86466357

Activity 3: Group Sharing

Ask the children, "Can you think of a time when a bad event turned out to be good and vice-versa?" Share with the group.

Activity 4: Unexpected Road Map Board Game

To make a board game, draw a winding path made up of many small boxes on a large poster board or large sheet of paper glued down to cardboard. Make different colored cut-out circles so each child has one. One end is the starting point, and the other end will be "A Shining Heart." (You will be able to use this board game again in the following chapters in a different way.) Then make several small cards of the same size. On each card write out a daily life happening which does not turn out as originally intended, both good and bad. Assign how many boxes each is worth, a number of steps forward or backward. Write on the cards examples like: the children whine because the picnic is cancelled, 2 steps back; the children are grateful when Mother makes a cake for them, 4 steps ahead. Making these cards will be a lesson in itself.

Before beginning the game, share the following *hadith* with the children: "How wonderful is the affair of the believer, for his affairs are all good, and this applies to no one but the believer. If something good happens to him, he is thankful for it and that is good for him. If something bad happens to him, he bears it with patience and that is good for him," (Muslim).

Have the children take turns choosing cards and reading off the story or scenario. In whatever box a child's colored spot lands, the child must recite a special *du'a'* from the *sunna* reported in *The Fortress of the Muslim* prayer book. If the result is pleasing, the child should say, in Arabic or English, "Alhamdu lillaahil-la<u>th</u>ee bini'matihi tatimmus-saalihaat," (Praise is to Allah Who by His blessings all good things are perfected). If the result is displeasing, the child should say, "Alhamdu lillaahi 'alaa kulli haal," (Praise is to Allah in all circumstances). Let your children take turns picking up a card until a winner finally reaches "The Shining Heart." If you have the time, ask the children to create the board and the game cards themselves to help reinforce the lessons they have been learning.

Activity 5: Sing Dawud Wharnsby's "The Ant"

Here is the link: https://www.youtube.com/watch?v=M_HA88qYYFk

"The Ant"

Oh little ant
I watch you below
I watch where you run
I watch where you go

Oh little ant
you carry a snack
as big as yourself
up there on your back

Oh little ant, you do struggle long
with a boulder crumb
but your faith so strong

Oh little ant
I learn from your way
to try though it's hard
being strong each day

Oh little ant
we're really both small
As I watch you
Allah's above us all

Activity 6: Guided Personal Reflection and Update Spiritual Heart Visual

Ask the children to spread out in the classroom with their Spiritual Heart Visual craft and/or journals. Ensure a serene environment perhaps with soft Islamic songs playing in background.

Provide a coloring sheet with one of the 99 Names ﷻ written in Arabic calligraphy. When beginning the reflection, the children can color this Name ﷻ. http://freecoloringpages.co.uk/?q=99%20allah%20names

Interchange coloring with free-drawing or other forms of art in future repetitions of this activity. (Ask the children to draw something that appealed to them in the lesson and to share the meanings behind their artwork later.)

Suggested Script:

1. Ask the Essential Question(s) of the chapter to the children, and allow them time to ponder upon their answers with their eyes closed or write it out in a personal journal.

2. Softly and kindly say something like this to the children: "Now close your eyes and focus on breathing in and out for 7 breaths repeating 'Al-' as one inhales and 'Hamdulilah' as one exhales. Try to find the deepest part inside your heart. Tell it that you wish to clean it and make it beautiful. Ask yourself everyday, 'Am I getting better?' Just focus on that answer being 'Yes.' Focus on getting better each day by sticking to good habits of thoughts, feelings, and actions. Don't worry about the far-off future just right now."

3. "Open your eyes and update your Spiritual Heart Visual removing any vices that you have avoided and keeping any vices that you are still trying to improve. Do not despair if vices remain—your intention is what matters!"

4. "Write down what you would like to improve and name at least one easy way that you can improve."

5. If possible, offer one-on-one time with each child to listen to their ideas and feelings about the class and daily activities, and reflect on their artwork.

Chapter Nineteen Curriculum Guidance

Core Lesson: The story about the boy losing the family horse expresses the importance of trusting Allah's ﷻ plan in all circumstances (*tawakul*).

Essential Question: Given that Allah ﷻ has always cared for me in the past, can I trust Allah's ﷻ plan for me now and in the future?

Activity 1: Connecting to the *Hadith*

Read to the children the following *hadith* and reflect upon its meaning. Ibn 'Umar reported that the Prophet Muhammad ﷺ said:

"When you pass by the gardens of Paradise, avail yourselves of them." The Companions asked: "What are the gardens of Paradise, O Messenger of Allah?" He replied: "The circles of *dhikr*. There are roaming angels of Allah who go about looking for the circles of *dhikr*, and when they find them they surround them closely," (Tirmidhi).

Activity 2: Seventy to One Treat Jar Craft: The aim of this game is to illustrate how one session of remembering God ﷻ is worth 70 periods of entertainment.

Suggested supplies:

Small candies, frosted almonds or any treat that can be counted out
Small glass jars
Art supplies to decorate the jars such as paint, construction paper, ribbons, glitter glue, etc.

Instruct the children to decorate a glass jar of treats. The children can write an inspirational message on the jar such as, "Always remember Allah ﷻ." Next have the children count out seventy treats and put them in their jar to take home to their families. Ask the children to hold one treat in their hand next to the jar full of treats and ask them, "Which do you prefer? Remembering Allah ﷻ once, or 70 times of play?" Tell the children to share the treats and teach about the reward of remembering Allah ﷻ with their family members at home.

Activity 3: Islamic Song Circle

Reward the children with a gathering of singing to celebrate their efforts and give thanks for everything they have learned so far. Serve special food and decorate the room with special memories such as pictures from their community service activities. You could also take a field trip to a campground or another special location. Gather in a circle and sing all the songs the children have learned so far, and other beautiful Islamic songs for children such as *"Tala al-badru alayna"*: https://www.youtube.com/watch?v=z5HiXM9JGJQ

Activity 4: Remember Allah ﷻ Always With Gratitude—Inspirational Short Film

There is a wonderful short film by a young Muslim girl that effectively explains a method of remembering Allah ﷻ in every moment of our lives. Please share with the children:

https://www.youtube.com/watch?v=TjHlxBBgDfg&feature=youtu.be

Activity 5: Family *Halaqa*

Gather your own children together once a week to read from the Quran, tell a story about the Prophet

Muhammad ﷺ, or any other form of remembrance. However, before you start, tell your children that you want the angels to see all of you remembering Allah ﷻ, so you will all remember Allah ﷻ together.

Activity 6: *Reminder* The Belongings of Paradise Charity Box

Schedule this day on your calendar so that the children are prepared and have chosen an item to bring into the classroom for the charity box. Remind the children something like, "While we do not bring any belongings from this life into Heaven, that's all right because the more good deeds we do in this life, Allah ﷻ will give us even better gifts and everlasting happiness in this world and Paradise."

Before the children put their donations into the box, ask them to remember using the item and how happy they felt at the time. Then ask them to explain why they don't use the item anymore. After they answer, explain to them again that these toys only bring happiness for a short period of time, but the actions that strengthen the spiritual heart will bring happiness in this world and the next.

Repeat this activity bi-weekly or monthly, and have the children take turns delivering the items to a chosen charity organization. We recommend that the children bring in only one item at a time so that they will have items to give in the future.

Activity 7: Secret Virtue Box

After allowing the children some time (recommended two weeks if possible) to practice their virtue, offer the Secret Virtue Box to each child so that a new virtue may be chosen, read, and noted, and then the slip of paper returned to the container. Remind the children of the Pearls of Wisdom, and talk positively to them about their efforts so far. You may choose to provide healthy treats around this time to make it pleasurable.

Chapter Twenty Curriculum Guidance

Core Lesson: If we join learning circles where God ﷻ is remembered, the angels attend and listen. Even one such session makes up for seventy times of distracting entertainment or wasted time.

Essential Question: Is remembering God ﷻ important in my life? Name one way I can do that.

Activity 1: Connecting to the Quran

Read to the children Surah 41 verse 30, and reflect upon its meaning:

"Lo! Those who say: Our Lord is Allah, and afterward are upright, the angels descend upon them, saying: Fear not nor grieve, but bear good tidings of the Paradise which ye are promised."

Also read the following *hadith qudsi*, and reflect upon its meaning with the children: "O son of Adam, so long as you call upon Me and ask of Me, I shall forgive you for what you have done, and I shall not mind. O son of Adam, were your sins to reach the clouds of the sky and were you then to ask forgiveness of Me, I would forgive you."

Activity 2: Dusty Mirror Experiment—Polishing our Heart Mirrors

Suggested supplies:

Hand-held mirror
Baby-powder or dust
Flashlight or lamp
Cleaning spray and towel for mirror

Involve the children in applying dust or baby powder to a hand-held mirror. Have one of the children shine the flashlight on the mirror or hold the mirror up to a light source. Ask them to take notes of what happens to the mirror. Now clean the mirror, and repeat. Ask the children, "What is different now?"

Activity 3: *Du'a'* for Forgiveness

Remind the children of the good news that asking for forgiveness is one of the ways to clean one's spiritual heart, and start anew. Teach the children to say a prayer for forgiveness to help clean away past dust. Here are two possibilities:

From *hadith*:

"Allaahumma anta rabbee, la ilaha illa anta, Khalaqtanee, wa ana abduka, wa ana ala ahdika wa wa'dika mastata'tu, a'outhu bika min sharri ma sanatu, aboo'u laka bini'matika alayya, wa aboo'u bitahmbee, faghfirlee fa'innahu la yaghfiru ath-thunooba 'illa 'anta" (Bukhari).

"O Allah, You are my Lord, there is none worthy of worship in truth except You. You created me and I am Your slave and I am abiding to Your covenant and promise as best as I can. I seek refuge in You from the evil that I have committed. I profess to You my sins and I acknowledge Your favor upon me, so forgive me verily no one forgives sins except You."

Activity 4: Forgiveness Notes

Ask the children to think of someone they may have hurt in the past. Do they feel sorry for it? Well, here is an opportunity to make it right, and make one's spiritual heart shine for doing so! Provide construction paper or blank notes and colored pencils for the children. Ask them to design notes in which they can ask for forgiveness from the person they hurt. Mention to the children how happy the person will be when they receive the note. Help the children send the note to the person or ask their parents to help them do so. It's all right if it is someone they live with. They can hide it under the person's pillow or put it on their seat at the dinner table.

Activity 5: Guided Personal Reflection and Update Spiritual Heart Visual

Ask the children to spread out in the classroom with their Spiritual Heart Visual craft and/or journals. Ensure a serene environment perhaps with soft Islamic songs playing in background.

Provide a coloring sheet with one of the 99 Names ﷻ written in Arabic calligraphy. When beginning the reflection, the children can color this Name ﷻ. http://freecoloringpages.co.uk/?q=99%20allah%20names

Interchange coloring with free-drawing or other forms of art in future repetitions of this activity. (Ask the children to draw something that appealed to them in the lesson and to share the meanings behind their artwork later.)

Suggested Script:

1. Ask the Essential Question(s) of the chapter to the children, and allow them time to ponder upon their answers with their eyes closed or write it out in a personal journal.

2. Softly and kindly say something like this to the children: "Now close your eyes and focus on breathing in and out for 7 breaths repeating 'Al-' as one inhales and 'Hamdulilah' as one exhales. Try to find the deepest part inside your heart. Tell it that you wish to clean it and make it beautiful. Ask yourself everyday, 'Am I getting better?' Just focus on that answer being 'Yes.' Focus on getting better each day by sticking to good habits of thoughts, feelings, and actions. Don't worry about the far-off future just right now."

3. "Open your eyes and update your Spiritual Heart Visual removing any vices that you have avoided and keeping any vices that you are still trying to improve. Do not despair if vices remain—your intention is what matters!"

4. "Write down what you would like to improve and name at least one easy way that you can improve."

5. If possible, offer one-on-one time with each child to listen to their ideas and feelings about the class and daily activities, and reflect on their artwork.

***

Teaching Methods for Chapter Twenty-One through Chapter Twenty-Nine

The next several chapters will hone in on most of the vices from the CAUTION List. We encourage you to use various fun games to get the children excited about this section. If you have been teaching alone, you might ask another adult to join you for these classes as "interactive skits" are an important part of the curriculum. Interactive skits involve two adults creating a short story to demonstrate the ugliness of poor character habits. Once the main story line has been acted out, the adults will alert the children to give their ideas on how to fix the situation. *Teach the children to ask questions first, and then give advice. The children should try to understand both sides of the story before coming up with solutions.* Go with the children's ideas (even if it wouldn't fix the situation entirely), and help guide them to instruct you to ask for forgiveness from Allah ﷻ and the other person, and then re-enact the scenario demonstrating the appropriate action.

The children will also be encouraged to make up their own interactive plays which they can perform for their teachers and classmates or simply play as games. Activities in the following sections will also be focused on remedies to the vices such as asking for forgiveness, forgiving others, secrets for protecting oneself from anger and arguing, and having gratitude.

Please continue with the daily Secret Virtue Box and Spiritual Heart Visual activities as constantly being aware of one's feelings, thoughts, and deeds should become a life habit. The Secret Virtue Box and Spiritual Heart Visual activities should now contain the corresponding virtues of the vices discussed in Chapters Twenty-One to Twenty-Nine. The nine vices to be discussed are envy, pride, back-biting, making excuses for yourself, bragging, prying and spying, not wanting the best for others, being two-faced/hypocrisy, and arguing. It is better to arrange the children's Spiritual Heart Visual and Secret Virtue Box slips to focus on just four or five vices and their corresponding virtues at one time.

Please also continue to support the children in serving others through their monthly community service projects. The group work and compassion needed to fulfill these activities are excellent opportunities to practice their assigned virtues.

Chapter Twenty-One and Chapter Twenty-Two Curriculum Guidance

Core Lesson for Chapter Twenty-One: We can think of our spiritual hearts like a heart that we have drawn right in front of us. Dots on the heart show problems that we need to correct because they harm our spiritual hearts.

Essential Questions for Chapter Twenty-One: What are "dots" on my spiritual heart that I would like to get rid of?

Core Lesson for Chapter Twenty-Two: To envy the blessings that God ﷻ gave to another, rather than to be grateful for one's own special blessings is very harmful. Envy eats up good deeds like fire devouring wood.

Essential Questions for Chapter Twenty-Two: Do I trust that God ﷻ has given to me and other people what we each need? Am I grateful? What should I say many times daily?

Activity 1: Connecting to the Quran and *Hadith*

Share the following *hadith*: Anas ibn Malik reported that Rasul Allah said, "Envy consumes good deeds just as fire burns wood. Charity extinguishes sinful deeds just as water extinguishes fire. Prayer is the light of the believer and fasting is his shield from the Hellfire." (Sunan Ibn Maja 4208).

Ask the children, "What behaviors does Allah ﷻ reward with blessings? Do the blessings have to be material? What are examples of non-material blessings?" and "What kind of behaviors would cause us to lose blessings or our past good deeds?"

Activity 2: Save My Good Deeds Skit

Suggested supplies:

The adults in the skit write out examples of past good deeds on construction paper such as "Prayed 5 times a day," "Fasted during Ramadan," "Cooked food for the poor," "Always told the truth," "Respected elders."

Waste basket lined with a clean bag (You can decorate the waste basket as a "fire" if desired.)

In this activity, the adults will make a skit in which they will start off as good friends working for the same goal, but then something happens making one friend envious of the other. Lay the cards of good deeds out in front so that the children can see them. Explain to them that these words represent the past good deeds of the envious adult. Assign each child a number. Tell them that if they notice any envious words or actions from the characters during the skit to walk up to the front in the order of their numbers and pick up a "past good deed" from the pile and drop it into the waste basket…because that is what happens to one's past good deeds when one is envious!

The purpose of giving the children assigned numbers is so that they do not all rush up at once to throw away the past good deeds. Tell the children that if they notice any envious speech or actions, but the next person in line has not yet noticed, they can kindly whisper a reminder into that person's ear. At the end of the skit, the envious friend will notice that all of his/her past good deeds are gone because of his/her envy, and he/she will feel remorseful and ask forgiveness from Allah ﷻ and the other friend. The remorseful actor can then win back their good deeds as a sign to the children that Allah ﷻ is Most Compassionate to those who seek forgiveness.

Post skit discussion points:

Does one really trust Allah ﷻ if he or she lets their envy take control of their reactions?

Do people display respect for Allah ﷻ if they envy others?

Can a person always stop the feeling of envy from coming up? What might we do when it does come up? We can *always* turn something negative into something positive. If we catch ourselves wanting what another has been blessed with, we can: a) be happy for our own special blessings, and b) be happy for the other's good fortune.

Activity 3: Gratitude Guess Who? Game

Ask each child to write down something they are grateful for with their name next to it on a slip of paper. Fold the slips of paper and put them into a container. Have each child take turns randomly picking a piece of paper and reading the item without saying the person's name. The group needs to guess who wrote the item. You can play this game multiple times with different themes such as "I am grateful for my mom/dad because…," "Even though some people may think this is a hardship, I am grateful for… because…," "I am grateful for the person sitting to my right because…," etc.

Activity 4: Gratitude Picture Game

Provide the children with colored pencils and medium-sized pieces of paper to make small drawings. Each child will have a turn drawing something they are grateful for while the group tries to guess! Rules include no words, letters, or numbers and a 60 second time limit to draw the picture. You can break the group up into teams or just have everyone play in one big team.

Activity 5: Thank You Notes

Provide blank notes, construction paper, and art supplies for the children and ask them to design thank you notes for special people in their lives. Ask them to be specific about what they are grateful for from that person as they write their notes. Assist the children in actually delivering the notes to the intended recipients.

Activity 6: Secret Virtue Box for Chapters Twenty-One to Twenty-Nine

Make the virtue slips in the Secret Virtue Box correspond to the vices in the Chapters you are teaching. Carry around the Secret Virtue Box to each child, and have them pick one or two slips of paper, read and note the virtues(s), and then return them to the container. Remind the children of the Pearls of Wisdom, and talk positively to them about their efforts so far. You may choose to provide treats around this time to make it pleasurable.

Activity 7: *Reminder* Serve Like the Prophet Muhammad ﷺ

Smile please! This is a friendly reminder to keep up the group charity projects scheduled on your Good Habit Calendar such as feeding the poor or visiting the elderly/sick. Remind the children to stay positive, put others before themselves, and TRY TO KEEP SMILING just like the beautiful smile of the Prophet Muhammad ﷺ! To put everyone in a light mood, have the children pair off for "smile contests"—whoever can smile the longest at another person wins a treat. (Hint: Let everyone win a treat in the end so that the children's spirits remain high.) Provide options to help the children handle any difficult feelings that come up such as one-on-one time with an adult mentor, quiet time, or ability to change activities.

Chapter Twenty-Three Curriculum Guidance

Core Lesson: Practicing humility instead of arrogance and kindness instead of meanness help to polish and protect the spiritual heart.

Essential Question: What can I do to make my character more humble?

Activity 1: Connecting to the Quran

Read Chapter 25 verses 63–64 to the children, and reflect upon its meaning:

"And the servants of the Infinitely Compassionate are those who walk on the earth in humility and when the ignorant address them they say, "Peace!"—those who spend the night in adoration of their Sustainer in prostration and standing upright."

Activity 2: I'm Better Than You—How Terrible! Skit

Develop a scenario and follow the guidelines for an interactive skit to be performed first by the adults. After you have helped guide the children to correct the grown-ups in the skit, ask them to create their own skits to demonstrate to the class or play together as a game. Here is an example of a skit/game that was submitted to Fons Vitae by a young girl:

Design a game where there are three small containers. One contains a small bag of treats while the others are empty. Randomly arrange the containers so that no one knows which contains the treats. Ask each child to pick a container. The child that picks the correct container will pretend to be arrogant, exclaiming gleefully that he/she is the best, calling himself/herself the winner. He/She can pretend to eat the candy while the other children sadly watch. Ask the children to talk about how they felt when the other person did not share and was acting arrogantly. Ask the winner to then demonstrate appropriate behavior by showing what humility looks like and sharing.

Activity 3: What Made Your Blessings Possible? Chain Exercise

Ask the children to list one blessing on top of a blank sheet of paper. Now ask the children, "What made this blessing possible?" (You will likely need to work one-on-one with students or ask students to help each other think about their blessings. You might decide to do one at a time if you're in a small group.) After they answer, ask again, "What made this blessing possible?" Repeat this question until a list of four or five worldly connections have been listed, and the children find that ultimately all blessings are from Allah ﷻ. Point out to the children how absurd it is to be arrogant when everything you have is connected to something or someone else, and it is all from Allah ﷻ anyway!

For example, a child lists "Going to a good school" as a blessing on top of their sheet of paper. She then draws an arrow down to "Because I was blessed with parents who can pay for it," and then draws an arrow down to "Because my parents have good jobs" and then draws an arrow down to "Because my parents studied hard in school while working part-time to support themselves" and then draws an arrow down to "Because my parents thought education was important" and then draws an arrow down to "Because in Islam we should seek knowledge" and then draws an arrow down to "Because the Prophet Muhammad ﷺ told us to do so" and then draws an arrow to "Because Allah ﷻ sent him as a Messenger ﷺ."

Activity 4: Valuing Each Other's Cultures Project

Read Surah 49 verse 13 to the children and reflect upon its meaning:

"O mankind! We created you from a single (pair) of a male and a female, and made you into nations and tribes, that ye may know each other (not that ye may despise each other). Verily the most honored of you in the sight of Allah is (he who is) the most righteous of you. And Allah has full knowledge and is well acquainted (with all things)."

In this project, ask the children to interview someone from another ethnic background about his/her culture and then prepare to present what they learned about that person's culture to the class. Give the children a list of five questions to answer about their own culture first. Then, to ask their interviewee:

1. What part of the world are you from? Find it on the map.

2. What languages do you speak?

3. What is an example of beautiful art or architecture in your culture?

4. Can you tell me a special short story from your culture's history or about a famous person in this history?

5. What are important values in your culture?

Activity 5: The Cure: Asking for Forgiveness

Remind the children of the good news that asking for forgiveness is one of the ways to clean one's spiritual heart, and start anew. Create another opportunity to write a note to another person asking for forgiveness by providing them with blank cards, construction paper, and colored pencils.

Did the children memorize the *du'a'*? Help them do so, and then reward them!

From *hadith*:

"Allaahumma anta rabbee, la ilaha illa anta, Khalaqtanee, wa ana abduka, wa ana ala ahdika wa wa'dika mastata'tu, a'outhu bika min sharri ma sanatu, aboo'u laka bini'matika alayya, wa aboo'u bitahmbee, faghfirlee fa'innahu la yaghfiru ath-thunooba 'illa 'anta," (Bukhari).

"O Allah You are my Lord, there is none worthy of worship in truth except You. You created me and I am Your slave and I am abiding to Your covenant and promise as best as I can. I seek refuge in You from the evil that I have committed. I profess to you my sins and I acknowledge Your favor upon me, so forgive me; verily no one forgives sins except you."

Activity 6: Guided Personal Reflection and Update Spiritual Heart Visual

Ask the children to spread out in the classroom with their Spiritual Heart Visual craft and/or journals. Ensure a serene environment perhaps with soft Islamic songs playing in background.

Provide a coloring sheet with one of the 99 Names ﷻ written in Arabic calligraphy. When beginning the reflection, the children can color this Name ﷻ. http://freecoloringpages.co.uk/?q=99%20allah%20names

Interchange coloring with free-drawing or other forms of art in future repetitions of this activity. (Ask the children to draw something that appealed to them in the lesson and to share the meanings behind their artwork later.)

Suggested Script:

1. Ask the Essential Question(s) of the chapter to the children, and allow them time to ponder upon their answers with their eyes closed or write it out in a personal journal.

2. Softly and kindly say something like this to the children: "Now close your eyes and focus on breathing in and out for 7 breaths repeating 'Al-' as one inhales and 'Hamdulilah' as one exhales. Try to find the deepest part inside your heart. Tell it that you wish to clean it and make it beautiful. Ask yourself everyday, 'Am I getting better?' Just focus on that answer being 'Yes.' Focus on getting better each day by sticking to good habits of thoughts, feelings, and actions. Don't worry about the far-off future just right now."

3. "Open your eyes and update your Spiritual Heart Visual removing any vices that you have avoided and keeping any vices that you are still trying to improve. Do not despair if vices remain—your intention is what matters!"

4. "Write down what you would like to improve and name at least one easy way that you can improve."

5. If possible, offer one-on-one time with each child to listen to their ideas and feelings about the class and daily activities, and reflect on their artwork.

Chapter Twenty-Four Curriculum Guidance

Core Lesson: Backbiting is so reprehensible that God ﷻ has compared it in the Quran to eating someone's dead body. Backbiting must never be done or even listened to, ever.

Essential Question: Would I like to eat someone's dead body? How can I win over the temptation to gossip?

Activity 1: Connecting to the Quran

For Chapter Twenty-Four and part of Chapter Twenty-Five, read to the children Surah 49 verse 12, and reflect upon its meaning:

"O ye who believe! Shun much suspicion; for lo! some suspicion is a crime. And spy not, neither backbite one another. Would one of you love to eat the flesh of his dead brother? Ye abhor that (so abhor the other)! And keep your duty (to Allah). Lo! Allah is Relenting, Merciful."

Activity 2: Interactive Skit for Backbiting

Here is an example of a skit you might use as a demonstration for the class, and one which the children can act out as well. Of course, feel free to make up your own. The children will have many good ideas.

1. Adults: Two friends sit together having fun discussing a new class they are taking together. Friend

A compliments the other person's shirt and asks where she got it from. Friend B answers that she got it from a second-hand store. Friend B now has to leave. Once gone, Friend A pretends to call a third friend on the phone and gossips about what she just discovered about Friend B.

2. Children: A teacher passes out the grades to the class. One person fails, while the other children pass. When the person who fails leaves, the other children begin to gossip about him/her.

Activity 3: Break Before You Backbite

As a part of the interactive skits or separately, teach the children to ask themselves four questions before they say anything about anyone. If the answer to any of these is "no" then it is likely backbiting or idle talk:

1. Will I be able to say this in front of the person I am talking about?

2. Am I absolutely sure that it is true?

3. Is what I am about to say kind?

4. Is what I am about to say necessary?

Activity 4: "The Power of Words" Demonstration

Inform the children that you will teach them about the "power of words" through a symbolic lesson. Carry a small bag of sand or another fine substance outside. Tell the children, "These grains of sand or salt are our words. We can use words to help people or to hurt people. They are very powerful." Sprinkle the sand/salt on the ground around you and look at it carefully. Now ask the children, "Pick up all the grains of sand, which are unkind words you have said against others. Can you get them back? Is it easy to take words back?"

Activity 5: Secret Virtue Box for Chapters Twenty-One to Twenty-Nine

Make the virtue slips in the Secret Virtue Box correspond to the vices in the Chapters you are teaching. Carry around the Secret Virtue Box to each child, and have them pick one or two slips of paper, read and note the virtues(s), and then return them to the container. Remind the children of the Pearls of Wisdom, and talk positively to them about their efforts so far. You may choose to provide treats around this time to make it pleasurable.

Activity 6: *Reminder* The Belongings of Paradise Charity Box

Schedule this day on your calendar so that the children are prepared and have chosen an item to bring into the classroom for the charity box. Remind the children something like, "While we do not bring any belongings from this life into Heaven, that's all right because the more good deeds we do in this life, Allah ﷻ will give us even better gifts and everlasting happiness in this world and Paradise."

Before the children put their donations into the box, ask them to remember using the item and how happy they felt at the time. Then ask them to explain why they don't use the item anymore. After they answer, explain to them again that these toys only bring happiness for a short period of time, but the actions that strengthen the spiritual heart will bring happiness in this world and the next.

Repeat this activity bi-weekly or monthly, and have the children take turns delivering the items to a chosen charity organization. We recommend that the children bring in only one item at a time so that they will have items to give in the future.

Chapter Twenty-Five Curriculum Guidance

Core Lessons: We need to make a habit of observing and correcting ourselves. The heart must be polished so it may reflect light and be able to understand higher and deeper ideas. Rather than making excuses and praising ourselves with words, we need to live and be those virtues, rather than say "ugly truths" by mentioning our own good deeds. Bragging and spying must be absolutely avoided.

Essential Questions: How do I feel when I am kind and forgiving? How do I feel when I brag?

Activity 1: Connecting to the Quran

For Chapter Twenty-Four and part of Chapter Twenty-Five, read to the children the following verses of the Quran and reflect upon their meanings:

Surah 49 verse 12: "O ye who believe! Shun much suspicion. Indeed, some suspicion is a crime…."

Surah 53 verse 33: "Do not justify yourselves. He knows very well who is pious (God-fearing)."

Activity 2: Interactive Skits

If needed, review the rules of an interactive skit in "Teaching Methods." Have the students create skits. Here are examples of scenarios for the adults or children to act out for the class as an interactive skit to which the group will respond and critique:

1. Spying:

   a. Character A tells Character B that he/she has a very important phone call to make. Character B asks "What is it for?" to which Character A answers "I'll tell you later." Character A then goes to a room and closes the door and gets on the phone. Character B then decides to try and listen behind the door to see what the conversation is about.

   b. Character A knows that Character B has been chosen to receive an award for memorizing the Quran. However, Character A thinks Character B doesn't deserve the award and plans to write a secret letter to the award committee telling them about all of Character B's bad character traits. Character A is following Character B around, and writing down everything naughty he/she does.

2. Bragging:

   a. A student comes home with an "A" on his/her test, and then starts bragging to his/her brothers and sisters about how he/she had the best grade in the class, how smart he/she is, and how others did not score as well.

   b. Two people meet for lunch, and Character A starts to exaggerate how tired he/she is. Character B asks about how Character A is doing, and Character A responds that he/she is so tired from staying up all night praying, cooking food for the poor, memorizing Quran, cleaning his/her big beautiful house…etc. Point out that bragging is sometimes done in very subtle ways! Mature students may be able to discuss, "Why do people brag?"

3. Making excuses:

   a. A student arrives late to class from recess, and the teacher tells him/her that he/she must stay for five minutes after school. The student begins to make up excuses for why the rule shouldn't apply to him/her, such as, "But I have the best grades in the class!", "But my daddy gave money to this school!", "But someone else tripped me, and I couldn't get up!"

Activity 3: Guided Personal Reflection and Update Spiritual Heart Visual

Ask the children to spread out in the classroom with their Spiritual Heart Visual craft and/or journals. Ensure a serene environment perhaps with soft Islamic songs playing in background.

Provide a coloring sheet with one of the 99 Names ﷻ written in Arabic calligraphy. When beginning the reflection, the children can color this Name ﷻ. http://freecoloringpages.co.uk/?q=99%20allah%20names

Interchange coloring with free-drawing or other forms of art in future repetitions of this activity. (Ask the children to draw something that appealed to them in the lesson and to share the meanings behind their artwork later.)

Suggested Script:

1. Ask the Essential Question(s) of the chapter to the children, and allow them time to ponder upon their answers with their eyes closed or write it out in a personal journal.

2. Softly and kindly say something like this to the children: "Now close your eyes and focus on breathing in and out for 7 breaths repeating 'Al-' as one inhales and 'Hamdulilah' as one exhales. Try to find the deepest part inside your heart. Tell it that you wish to clean it and make it beautiful. Ask yourself everyday, 'Am I getting better?' Just focus on that answer being 'Yes.' Focus on getting better each day by sticking to good habits of thoughts, feelings, and actions. Don't worry about the far-off future just right now."

3. "Open your eyes and update your Spiritual Heart Visual removing any vices that you have avoided and keeping any vices that you are still trying to improve. Do not despair if vices remain—your intention is what matters!"

4. "Write down what you would like to improve and name at least one easy way that you can improve."

5. If possible, offer one-on-one time with each child to listen to their ideas and feelings about the class and daily activities, and reflect on their artwork.

Chapter Twenty-Six Curriculum Guidance

Core Lessons: It is not easy to do, but it is important to learn how to wish the best for others and not secretly be pleased with their failings.

Essential Question: Can I be a great enough person to wish the best for others?

Activity 1: Connecting to the *Hadith*

Read this *hadith* to the children, and reflect upon its meaning: Anas relates that the Prophet Muhammad ﷺ said: "None of you truly believes until he loves for his brother what he loves for himself," (Bukhari and Muslim).

Activity 2: Making My Heart Gold—Practice the Golden Rule Today!

Ask the children to think of someone they know who is trying to accomplish a goal or who has been struggling with something. Once they have someone in mind, ask the children to draw a heart and color it gold. Inside of the heart, ask them to write down one way they could help that person achieve what they want or improve. It's all right if the ideas for helping are very simple. Just try to make the items as specific as possible. Ask the children, "Will this help to give you a heart of gold?" Ask the children to share with you their ideas so that you can assist them in accomplishing the goal of helping the other person. Include their artwork in their journals or post it in your classroom.

Activity 3: "Breaking News: This Just In!"—Reporting Our Blessings Game

Ask the children to pretend that they are news reporters with an assignment to collect stories about other people's blessings to present on the evening news. Emphasize that the goal is to report other people's blessings joyfully and happily as if the blessings were their own! Break the children up into groups if possible. Ask the children to share stories from their own lives with each other or interview their teachers for ideas about stories. Give the children time to plan their presentation. Arrange the room so that the presenters can sit at a desk in the front of the room. Optional: Offer to record the presentations for their parents and for future reminiscing.

Activity 4: *Golden Rule Special* Secret Virtue Box for Chapters Twenty-One to Twenty-Nine

Make the virtue slips in the Secret Virtue Box correspond to the vices in the chapters you are teaching, with special emphasis on the Golden Rule. Carry around the Secret Virtue Box to each child, and have them pick one or two slips of paper, read and note the virtue(s), and then return them to the container. Together, discuss ideas about how to be aware of the Golden Rule while practicing their virtues. Every time they practice a virtue, everyone should try to think of why it is connected to the Golden Rule.

Activity 5: *Reminder* Serve Like the Prophet Muhammad ﷺ

Smile please! This is a friendly reminder to keep up the group charity projects scheduled on your Good Habit Calendar such as feeding the poor, visiting the elderly/sick, or even picking up trash. Remind the children to stay positive, put others before themselves, and TRY TO KEEP SMILING just like the beautiful smile of the Prophet Muhammad ﷺ! To put everyone in a light mood, have the children pair off for "smile contests"—whoever can smile the longest at another person wins a treat. (Hint: Let everyone win a treat in the end so that the children's spirits remain high.) Provide options to help the children handle any difficult feelings that come up such as one-on-one time with an adult mentor, quiet time, or ability to change activities.

Chapter Twenty-Seven Curriculum Guidance

Core Lesson: Hypocrisy is one of the most harmful vices, the one whose gravity drove al-Ghazali from his teaching profession. We must be and act in the same way we advise others. We must be the same person for everyone we meet.

Essential Question: Do I ever tell a lie or break a promise? Do I say I have done something I have not done?

Activity 1: Connecting to the Quran and *Hadith*:

Read Surah 4 verse 142 to the children and reflect upon its meaning:

"The Hypocrites—they think they are over-reaching God, but He will over-reach them: When they stand up to prayer, they stand without earnestness, to be seen of men, but little do they hold God in remembrance."

Next, read to the children the following *hadith*, and include these examples in your next Secret Virtue Box:

"The signs of the hypocrite are three: when he speaks he lies, when he promises he breaks his promise, and when he is entrusted he betrays the trust," (Bukhari and Muslim).

Activity 2: Interactive Skits

If needed, review the rules of an interactive skit in "Teaching Methods." Here are examples of scenarios for the adults or children to act out for the class as an interactive skit which everyone can discuss. Create your own.

1. Hypocrisy:

   a. Two children are playing at school. Child A has a toy that Child B wants to play with. Child A refuses to share, and Child B says "You should share your toys!" and then gets up to go home. When Child B arrives home, he/she refuses to share his/her toys with siblings.

   b. Child A is organizing a charity to give food to poor people, and he/she is speaking in front of a group of people asking them to donate money. People are praising him/her. Later at home, Child A is eating dinner when a neighbor calls him/her to say he/she is hungry and doesn't have food. Child A hangs up on his/her neighbor.

Activity 3: Spiritual Heart Guided Reflection and Update Spiritual Heart Visual

Ask the children to spread out in the classroom with their Spiritual Heart Visual craft and/or journals. Ensure a serene environment perhaps with soft Islamic songs playing in background.

Provide a coloring sheet with one of the 99 Names ﷻ written in Arabic calligraphy. When beginning the reflection, the children can color this Name ﷻ. http://freecoloringpages.co.uk/?q=99%20allah%20names

Interchange coloring with free-drawing or other forms of art in future repetitions of this activity. (Ask the children to draw something that appealed to them in the lesson and to share the meanings behind their artwork later.)

Suggested Script:

1. Ask the Essential Question(s) of the chapter to the children, and allow them time to ponder upon their answers with their eyes closed or write it out in a personal journal.

2. Softly and kindly say something like this to the children: "Now close your eyes and focus on breathing in and out for 7 breaths repeating 'Al-' as one inhales and 'Hamdulilah' as one exhales. Try to find the deepest part inside your heart. Tell it that you wish to clean it and make it beautiful. Ask yourself everyday, 'Am I getting better?' Just focus on that answer being 'Yes.' Focus on getting better each day by sticking to good habits of thoughts, feelings, and actions. Don't worry about the far-off future just right now."

3. "Open your eyes and update your Spiritual Heart Visual removing any vices that you have avoided and keeping any vices that you are still trying to improve. Do not despair if vices remain—your intention is what matters!"

4. "Write down what you would like to improve and name at least one easy way that you can improve."

5. If possible, offer one-on-one time with each child to listen to their ideas and feelings about the class and daily activities, and reflect on their artwork.

Chapter Twenty-Eight Curriculum Guidance

Core Lesson: Arguing and quarreling are bad for those engaged in it, and miserable for those looking on. Imam al-Ghazali mentions a tradition in which we are told that God ﷻ builds a house in Paradise for those who stop arguing, especially when they are in the wrong. But for those who stop arguing when they are in the right, that house will be placed for them in the highest part of heaven.

Essential Questions: Can I be strong enough not to argue? How does it feel after I have avoided an argument? How does it feel after I have argued, even if I won?

Activity 1: Connecting to the Quran

Read to the children Surah 17 verse 53, and reflect upon its meaning:

"And tell my servants that they should speak in a kind manner, for truly Satan is ready to stir up discord between people."

Activity 2: "The Power of Words" Demonstration

If not already done in Chapter Twenty-Four, inform the children that you will teach them about the "power of words" through a symbolic lesson. Carry a small bag of sand or another fine substance outside. Tell the children, "These grains of sand or salt are our words. We can use words to help people or to hurt people. They are very powerful." Sprinkle the sand/salt on the ground around you and look at them carefully. Now ask the children, "Can you pick up the sand/salt and put it back in the bag? Even if you are able to collect some of it, are you able to collect all of it? If not, why? How does this relate to the words we speak? Is it easy to take words back?"

Activity 3: Invisible to Us, but Loved So Much: the Prophet Muhammad ﷺ

This is an incredibly beautiful short film about a young French boy who is asked to draw the Prophet Muhammad ﷺ. His response is breathtaking and it teaches us about how to love and recognize Rasul Allah ﷺ in our own lives, and also how to respond to negativity with something better. Ask the children to reflect upon how the young boy responded, and why it made such a big impact on his teacher. Here is the link: http://themuslimvibe.com/videos/from-the-web/a-muslim-student-is-asked-to-draw-prophet-muhammad-his-response-is-breathtakingly-beautiful-video/

Activity 4: Prayer to Avoid Anger

Bring the children the good news that there is a prayer to ward off anger that may lead to arguing. You may have the children memorize it for a small reward.

"A'oothu billaahi minash-Shaytaanir-rajeem"

Activity 5: Hasan and Hossein's Winning Method

Share with the children the story of Hasan and Hossein (may Allah ﷺ eternally bless them) in which the two boys saw an older man making ablutions incorrectly. Instead of scolding him, they asked him to watch each of them make *wudu* and be a judge as to who made *wudu* the best. In this way, the man realized his own mistakes without being humiliated. Ask the children to act out this scenario, and come up with different ways in which they could gently teach someone who was doing something incorrectly the proper way of making *wudu*. Then have them do it in an impolite manner and ask them how it felt.

Next ask the children to use the same method of gentleness to avoid arguing in a pretend scenario. Some ideas for pretend scenarios:

1. Two children are playing tennis. One person hits the ball, and the other person says that the ball landed out of bounds.
2. A family is going on a trip. Two siblings both want to sit in the front seat.

Activity 6: A Game of Charades to Clarify Vices and Virtues

Recap on all the vices and virtues you have covered so far by writing them out on small pieces of paper of the same size. Divide the children into two teams or play as one group. If breaking the group into teams, one player from each team will choose a card and show it to the other team. He/She will then try to act out the virtue/vice to their own team who will try to guess it.

One minute is usually sufficient to guess, but you may alter the time limit. The actor may not speak words or silently pronounce them, but can make other sounds. Allowing the use of props will make it easier to guess. You should let the guessers know when they have guessed correctly. If any of the guessers says the correct word within the time limit, then their team wins a point. If not, the other team wins a point. Alternate until each team member has had an opportunity to be an actor or all virtues/vices have been covered.

Activity 7: Steps to Paradise—Refusing Vices

This is just like activity "f." in the Workbook. As a review of the CAUTION List, use the image of stairs in the Workbook or have the children draw or create their own picture of a flight of stairs to heaven. On each step, have the children write out, "I refuse to envy," "I refuse to brag," "I refuse to argue," etc. covering all the vices you have discussed. If creating their own picture, count out the vices you want them

177

to include and tell them ahead of time the number of steps to include.

Activity 8: Secret Virtue Box for Chapters Twenty-One to Twenty-Nine

Make the slips in the Secret Virtue Box correspond to the vices in the chapters you are teaching. Carry around the Secret Virtue Box to each child, and have them pick one or two slips of paper, read and note the virtues(s), and then return them to the container. Remind the children of the Pearls of Wisdom, and talk positively to them about their efforts so far. You may choose to provide treats around this time to make it pleasurable.

Chapter Twenty-Nine Curriculum Guidance

Core Lesson: Imam al-Ghazali mentions that among the people of learning there are three kinds. This first group only cares for this world and its pleasures; the second teach special knowledge and are themselves humble servants and examples of what they share; the last group—in which most people are to be found—are those who know about and teach the highest ideas but hypocritically do not practice what they preach.

Essential Question: Can I find the strength inside of me to practice what I know?

Activity 1: Connecting to the Quran

Read to the children Surah 4 verse 145, and reflect upon its meaning in relation to the three groups mentioned by Imam al-Ghazali:

"Verily, the hypocrites will be in the lowest depth (grade) of the Fire; no helper will you find for them."

Activity 2: "The Path to My Shining Heart" Board Game

To make a board game, draw a winding path made up of several small boxes on a large poster board or large sheet of paper glued down to cardboard. At one end will be the starting point, and the other end will be "A Shining Heart." Then make several small cards. On each card write down a vice/virtue and how many boxes it is worth. Incorporate lessons from the three groups mentioned in Chapter Twenty-Nine such as, "Praying so that others can think you're a good person—move back 3 boxes," or "Trying to get really rich so you can show off—move back 2 boxes," and "Praying on time for God's ﷻ sake alone—move up 3 boxes." (Try to reinforce the idea that hypocritical actions receive the worst punishment.)

If the children are younger, you can keep the cards very simple such as, "Sharing your toys—move up 2 boxes," or "Talking back to your Mom—move back 2 boxes," "Hitting other children—move back one box." Let your children take turns choosing a card until they finally reach "The Shining Heart." If you have the time, ask the children to create the board and the game cards themselves to help reinforce the lessons they have been learning!

Activity 3: My Life Book

In this craft, the children will learn a surprising truth about their lives: that everything they feel, think, and do can be recorded in their "Life Book." Just like a famous author writes an amazing story that the reader loves to read, each of us is also trying to write an amazingly beautiful life story in our "Life Book." Provide the children with folded together pieces of card stock paper, construction paper, blank stationary, or a blank children's books (which can be bought at craft stores or online). They may also use a page in their journal. The children will write the life story they would want Allah ﷻ to read about them. Depending on the age of the children, they may need one-on-one assistance to write in a story-like format. Illustrations are welcome.

The following is an example: Maryam Nur was born on January 10th, 2004, to her mother and father. As a little girl she loved to…As she grew up she learned to…"help the poor by making food for them"… "always tell the truth"…Sometimes Maryam struggled because…"it was hard to share"…"other children teased her and she became upset"…but she learned to overcome this by…"loving to make other people happy"…"forgiving other people." When she grew up she became a…"scholar of Islam"…"doctor"… "fireman"… She helped everyone around her by…She was known to be…"kind," "helpful," "humble." She lived her life in service of Allah ﷻ.

Activity 4: Children's Poem to accompany "My Life Book"

Incorporate poetry into your classroom by simply reading a poem to the children, writing it out beautifully on the cover of their "My Life Book" craft, or even have them memorize it. Shaykh Abdal Hakim Murad has published a wonderful children's book with classical Islamic poetry for children entitled *Montmorency's Book of Rhymes*. Simply read the poem below and attribute it to the author (from p. 93 of the book):

"In Allah's ﷻ great Book, where but angels look
On pages of spotless beauty,
Are written in letters of living light
A Muslim's life and his duty"

Activity 5: Guided Personal Reflection and Update Spiritual Heart Visual

Ask the children to spread out in the classroom with their Spiritual Heart Visual craft and/or journals. Ensure a serene environment perhaps with soft Islamic songs playing in background.

Provide a coloring sheet with one of the 99 Names ﷻ written in Arabic calligraphy. When beginning the reflection, the children can color this Name ﷻ. http://freecoloringpages.co.uk/?q=99%20allah%20names

Interchange coloring with free-drawing or other forms of art in future repetitions of this activity. (Ask the children to draw something that appealed to them in the lesson and to share the meanings behind their artwork later.)

Suggested Script:

1. Ask the Essential Question(s) of the chapter to the children, and allow them time to ponder upon their answers with their eyes closed or write it out in a personal journal.

2. Softly and kindly say something like this to the children: "Now close your eyes and focus on breathing in and out for 7 breaths repeating 'Al-' as one inhales and 'Hamdulilah' as one exhales. Try to find the deepest part inside your heart. Tell it that you wish to clean it and make it beautiful. Ask yourself everyday, 'Am I getting better?' Just focus on that answer being 'Yes.' Focus on getting better each day by sticking to good habits of thoughts, feelings, and actions. Don't worry about the far-off future just right now."

3. "Open your eyes and update your Spiritual Heart Visual removing any vices that you have avoided and keeping any vices that you are still trying to improve. Do not despair if vices remain—your intention is what matters!"

4. "Write down what you would like to improve and name at least one easy way that you can improve."

5. If possible, offer one-on-one time with each child to listen to their ideas and feelings about the class and daily activities, and reflect on their artwork.

Activity 6: *Reminder* The Belongings of Paradise Charity Box

Schedule this day on your calendar so that the children are prepared and have chosen an item to bring into the classroom for the charity box. Remind the children something like, "While we do not bring any belongings from this life into Heaven, that's all right because the more good deeds we do in this life, Allah ﷻ will give us even better gifts and everlasting happiness in this world and Paradise."

Before the children put their donations into the box, ask them to remember using the item and how happy they felt at the time. Then ask them to explain why they don't use the item anymore. After they answer, explain to them again that these toys only bring happiness for a short period of time, but the actions that strengthen the spiritual heart will bring happiness in this world and the next.

Repeat this activity bi-weekly or monthly, and have the children take turns delivering the items to a chosen charity organization. We recommend that the children bring in only one item at a time so that they will have items to give in the future.

Chapter Thirty Curriculum Guidance

Core Lesson: Imam al-Ghazali's uses a metaphor of the heart housing angels who are frightened away by bad thoughts. He compares bad thoughts to barking dogs. He explains that when an angel finds a heart empty—polished and pure of its own concerns—even for a brief moment, it settles there.

Essential Question: Will I welcome the angels into my heart or leave the barking dogs there?

Activity 1: Connecting to the Quran

Read to the children Surah 2 verse 22, and reflect upon its meaning:

"For Allah loves those who turn to Him constantly and He loves those who keep themselves pure and clean."

Activity 2: Clean for the Angels

Ask the children to pretend that their rooms at home are like their hearts. Ask them to clean their rooms so that an angel would like to come. Explain how this is similar to polishing their hearts.

Activity 3: My Heart is Clean, Dear Angels! Connecting to the *Hadith*

Share this *hadith* with the children:

The Messenger of Allah ﷺ was sitting with a group of the Companions ﷺ in the *masjid* and he said, "A man will now enter (who is) from the people of Paradise," and a Companion walked in. Later it happened again, and then a third time. 'Abdullah ibn 'Amr ibn al-'Aas ﷺ wanted to find out what was so special about this man, so he asked the man if he might stay over at his house for three days. (He made up an excuse.) The man allowed him to stay. 'Abdullah noticed that the man didn't do anything out of the ordinary: He didn't fast all the time, he slept some of the night and prayed some of the night, and so on. So after the three days, 'Abdullah told him the real reason why he had requested to stay with him. He asked him what it was that could be the reason why he was from the people of *Jannah*. The man couldn't think of anything, but after a bit he said, "Every night, before I go to sleep, I forgive whoever has wronged me. I remove any bad feelings towards anyone from my heart" (Musnad Ahmad).

Emphasize to the children that the angels must have loved to visit this Companion ﷺ because he removed dirty feelings and deeds from his spiritual heart. Now share this wise saying:

Hamdun al-Qassar, one of the great early Muslims, said, "If a friend among your friends errs, make seventy excuses for him. If your hearts are unable to do this, then know that the shortcoming is in your own selves," (Imam Bayhaqi, *Shu'ab al-Iman*, 7.522).

Guide the children through this reflection to help clean the spiritual heart:

1. Think of someone whom you are feeling upset with. What did that person do? Can you think of seventy excuses for this person? Begin to think of good reasons why he may have acted in a certain way.

2. After making just a few excuses for him, maybe you are beginning to think this person deserves forgiveness? If you forgive others, Allah ﷻ will forgive you, and send His angels to you.

3. Can you forgive them? Silently repeat to yourself, "Dear (person's name), I forgive you for…Please forgive me for anyway that I have hurt you. And Dear Allah ﷻ, please forgive me too. Ameen."

Ask the children to begin practicing this exercise at night. Include "forgiving others" in the Secret Virtue Box.

Activity 4: *Reminder* Serve Like the Prophet Muhammad ﷺ

This is a friendly reminder to keep up the group charity projects scheduled on your Good Habit Calendar such as feeding the poor or visiting the elderly/sick. Perhaps you could pick up trash in places like the park. Remind the children to stay positive, put others before themselves, and TRY TO KEEP SMILING just like the beautiful smile of the Prophet Muhammad ﷺ! To put everyone in a light mood, have the children pair off for "smile contests"—whoever can smile the longest at another person wins a treat. (Hint: Let everyone win a treat in the end so that the children's spirits remain high.) Provide options to help the children handle any difficult feelings that come up, such as one-on-one time with an adult mentor, quiet time, or changing activities.

Activity 5: Secret Virtue Box Special Edition

Let the children know that this week you will be adding the special virtue of forgiving others to the Secret Virtue Box. Remind the children that they can practice this virtue all the time and especially right before sleeping at night.

Chapter Thirty-One Curriculum Guidance

Core Lesson: Time could be compared to a stream carrying water to nourish a paradisal garden but easily diverted and used up along the way. One must order one's time to be sure beautiful doings are planned at regular times. Time runs out faster than one thinks.

Essential Question: What things am I doing daily that may be distracting me from doing a good deed like helping my mother?

Activity 1: Connecting to the Quran

Read to the children Surah 2 verse 152, and reflect upon its meaning:

"Therefore remember Me, I will remember you. Give thanks to Me, and reject not Me."

Activity 2: Caring for Four Plants

Follow the activity suggested in the Workbook.

Activity 3: "No One is a Good Multi-tasker" Demonstration

In this activity, the children will be asked to complete a project in just three minutes while multi-tasking. They will then be asked to focus on completing just one task in three minutes. For example, present each child with three coloring pages and tell them to color all three pages in just three minutes. (The product will be messy or incomplete.) Then present each child with just one brand new coloring page and ask them to color it within three minutes. Compare the results with the children. Make the point that the days of our lives are also limited just like the time allotted for this activity. If we focus on too many things, we will not do anything well. If we focus on just the most important, we will succeed, God-willing.

Another way to demonstrate how multi-tasking hinders success is to play a game of tossing a ball back and forth in a group. After tossing just one ball back and forth for a few minutes, continue to add more and more balls to the group until everyone is overwhelmed and unable to pass and catch without dropping any balls. Reflect on the experience with the children.

Activity 4: Check-in: Freeing Up Time for Good Deeds

Guide the children through these questions:

1. Name three things that you like to do when you are not in school.

2. When do you do these activities and for how long? Which is the least important to you, and would you be willing to do something better instead?

3. Make a plan to spend less time doing one of these activities so that you have an extra 30 minutes to build good habits each day. For example, "I will spend 30 minutes less playing computer games each day so that I can help my little brother with his math homework."

4. Write notes to yourself to take 30 minutes each day to practice a new good habit, and stick them in the places that you did the old activities and on your bathroom mirror as a reminder.

Activity 5: Memorize Surah al-Asr

As one of the shortest Surahs in the Quran, and often one of the first taught to children, help the children to memorize Surah al-Asr for a small reward (such as the new daily planner mentioned below). Emphasize that this is an excellent Surah to recite when they feel they do not have enough time to stop and pray to Allah ﷻ. Also reflect upon its meaning: "By time, indeed, mankind is in loss, except for those who have believed and done righteous deeds and advised each other to truth and advised each other to patience."

Activity 6: "Planning For My Heart" Craft

If not already done, reward the children with their own brand new daily planners. Provide art materials for the children to decorate the outside cover of their journals with an inspirational message about the true meaning of life. Covering their decorated covers with clear contact paper or tape will protect their designs.

Teach the children a "secret to success" in planning their day around their five daily prayers. If they have an idea about what they will be doing from one prayer to the next, it helps them meet those goals as well as avoid missing a prayer.

Activity 7: Spiritual Heart Guided Personal Reflection and Update Spiritual Heart Visual

Ask the children to spread out in the classroom with their Spiritual Heart Visual craft and/or journals. Ensure a serene environment perhaps with soft Islamic songs playing in background.

Provide a coloring sheet with one of the 99 Names ﷻ written in Arabic calligraphy. When beginning the reflection, the children can color this Name ﷻ. http://freecoloringpages.co.uk/?q=99%20allah%20names

Interchange coloring with free-drawing or other forms of art in future repetitions of this activity. (Ask the children to draw something that appealed to them in the lesson and to share the meanings behind their artwork later.)

Suggested Script:

1. Ask the Essential Question(s) of the chapter to the children, and allow them time to ponder upon their answers with their eyes closed or write it out in a personal journal.

2. Softly and kindly say something like this to the children: "Now close your eyes and focus on breathing in and out for 7 breaths repeating 'Al-' as one inhales and 'Hamdulilah' as one exhales. Try to find the deepest part inside your heart. Tell it that you wish to clean it and make it beautiful. Ask yourself everyday, 'Am I getting better?' Just focus on that answer being 'Yes.' Focus on getting better each day by sticking to good habits of thoughts, feelings, and actions. Don't worry about the far-off future just right now."

3. "Open your eyes and update your Spiritual Heart Visual removing any vices that you have tried to avoid and keeping any vices that you are still trying to improve. Do not despair if vices remain—your intention is what matters!"

4. "Write down what you would like to improve and name at least one easy way that you can improve."

5. If possible, offer one-on-one time with each child to listen to their ideas and feelings about the class and daily activities, and reflect on their artwork.

Chapter Thirty-Two Curriculum Guidance

Core Lesson: We must be humble, empty, and ready to learn from experienced teachers who are truly "saving" ours lives by nourishing our spiritual growth, just as rain restores the dry earth.

Essential Question: Can I be brave enough to welcome Real Learning into my life even if it challenges my prior beliefs?

Activity 1: Connecting to the Quran

Read to the children Surah 78 part of verse 178, and reflect upon its meaning:

"He whom God guides, he alone is truly guided: whereas those whom He lets go astray-it is they, they who are the losers!…"

Activity 2: "Thank you" Cards for those Who Teach You

Each child is asked to draw a lion on his or her card, recalling the lion in the workbook who escaped from his zoo cage. Before he gobbled up anyone, someone saved the children's lives. In the note, the child can explain that she is thankful for being taught Real Learning, saving her from wasting her life, and showing special ways to Heaven.

Activity 3: "Open to Receive Knowledge" Demonstration

Make some lemonade or another beverage in a pitcher. Count how many children will be present and place the same amount of cups at the table ahead of time. Fill them with water. Now invite the children to join you at the table for a drink. Once they arrive and notice that the cups are already full of water, begin to pour a little bit of lemonade into one of the full cups. Have napkins ready. Explain to the children, "This is like a child or student who thinks he/she already has so much knowledge that he/she has nothing left to learn from his/her parent or teacher. All of this good knowledge just got wasted because the student came to class not open to receiving new knowledge." Now pour the water in each of the cups back into another container (so as not to waste it), and into empty cups pour lemonade for the children. Say something like, "May each of you be open to receiving a wonderful message that will bring you much joy and happiness."

Activity 4: The Ocean of Knowledge Activity

Keep the children's spirits high by arranging for them to go swimming at an indoor or outdoor pool or a natural body of water. Share Surah 31 verse 27:

"And if all the trees in the earth were pens, and the sea with seven more seas added to it (were ink), the words of Allah would not be exhausted. Surely Allah is Mighty, Wise."

Bring along clear containers of different sizes to symbolically demonstrate learning from the "ocean of knowledge" like the scholar who has received from the endless knowledge of Allah ﷻ. You could do the "Open to Receive Knowledge Demonstration" at this location as well.

Activity 5: Kneading My Heart

Divide the children into two groups. Give one group new containers of soft play dough and the other group old containers of relatively hardened play dough. Ask the children to create something beautiful such as flowers, stars, etc. Only the soft play dough will allow for this. Say to the children: "Soft hearts are open to new ideas, and they can become more beautiful because of it. However, hard hearts miss out on the chance to learn and become beautiful. The children can end this activity by doing something fun with the play dough, such as creating a group sculpture.

Activity 6: Secret Virtue Box

After allowing the children some time (recommended two weeks if possible) to practice their virtue, offer the Secret Virtue Box to each child so that a new virtue may be chosen, read, and noted, and then the slip of paper returned to the container. Remind the children of the Pearls of Wisdom, and talk positively to them about their efforts so far. You may choose to provide healthy treats around this time to make it pleasurable.

Chapter Thirty-Three Curriculum Guidance

Special Note: Revisit the Pearls of Wisdom as necessary to encourage the children to be proud of their efforts as every small step brings us closer to Allah ﷻ. Learning good habits takes time, and it may be necessary to revisit a previous step.

Core Lesson: We need to aim at a clear destination or target with our studies and daily lives, while establishing a solid foundation on which to build.

Essential Question: What are my targets in this life? What goals am I hoping to reach?

Activity 1: Connecting to the Quran

Read to children Surah 51 verse 56, and reflect upon its meaning:

"I have only created Jinn and men, that they may serve Me."

Activity 2: Start in the Right Place Demonstration

For this activity, you can use any item that needs assembling and has instructions. Something child-like, like Legos, would be more appealing but it is not necessary. Ask your children to try and make a model by starting from the middle of the instructions. Once they realize that it is too difficult or will lead to problems, you can kindly remind them that seeking knowledge is the same way; you must start from the beginning, build a strong foundation, and build upon it in the right order. Now start from the beginning and finish the model. Or perhaps a model could be made from blocks.

In addition, you can demonstrate this point by asking the children to take a look at a math textbook (preferably one that they are studying). Flip to the last few chapters and ask them if they understand it. Then explain to them that the later chapters are meant to be more difficult. However, the good news is that one doesn't start at the end, but starts at the beginning in order to prepare for the later chapters. Once one completes a chapter with a teacher who is there to help, then he/she can move on to the next chapter. You can also demonstrate this point with a *tajweed* (arabic pronunciation) book.

Activity 3: Target: Closeness to Allah ﷻ Craft

Suggested materials:

Cardboard, foam board, or cork
Colored contact paper, felt, or construction paper
Strong glue, with adult supervision only
Scissors
Velcro tape
Large craft ring (optional)

Dart options include nerf darts, pencils with short nails taped to the top, or small balls if no other item is available

Cut the sturdier board into a circle using the craft ring or other circular item (such as a bucket) as a guide. Glue the lighter material to the top for decoration and add a cutout of a "shining heart" to the center. Add an inspirational message about our goal in life such as, "Closeness to Allah ﷻ" to the board or above the board. Apply the Velcro tape as desired (optional). Nerf darts, pencils with short nails taped to the top, or balls may be used as darts. Many other examples of do-it-yourself dart boards can be found online.

Activity 4: Target: Closeness to Allah ﷻ Game

Research if archery is a possibility in your location. If not, you can use the dart board craft above. Play a few rounds of target practice with the children. Keep it light-hearted and fun, but give a gentle reminder about the real target in life.

Activity 5: *Reminder* The Belongings of Paradise Charity Box

Schedule this day on your calendar so that the children are prepared and have chosen an item to bring into the classroom for the charity box. Remind the children something like, "While we do not bring any belongings from this life into Heaven, that's all right because the more good deeds we do in this life, Allah ﷻ will give us even better gifts and everlasting happiness in this world and Paradise."

Before the children put their donations into the box, ask them to remember using the item and how happy they felt at the time. Then ask them to explain why they don't use the item anymore. After they answer, explain to them again that these toys only bring happiness for a short period of time, but the actions that strengthen the spiritual heart will bring happiness in this world and the next.

Repeat this activity bi-weekly or monthly, and have the children take turns delivering the items to a chosen charity organization. We recommend that the children bring in only one item at a time so that they will have items to give in the future.

Activity 6: Guided Personal Reflection and Update Spiritual Heart Visual

Ask the children to spread out in the classroom with their Spiritual Heart Visual craft and/or journals. Ensure a serene environment perhaps with soft Islamic songs playing in background.

Provide a coloring sheet with one of the 99 Names ﷻ written in Arabic calligraphy. When beginning the reflection, the children can color this Name ﷻ. http://freecoloringpages.co.uk/?q=99%20allah%20names

Interchange coloring with free-drawing or other forms of art in future repetitions of this activity. (Ask the children to draw something that appealed to them in the lesson and to share the meanings behind their artwork later.)

Suggested Script:

1. Ask the Essential Question(s) of the chapter to the children, and allow them time to ponder upon their answers with their eyes closed or write it out in a personal journal.

2. Softly and kindly say something like this to the children: "Now close your eyes and focus on breathing in and out for 7 breaths repeating 'Al-' as one inhales and 'Hamdulilah' as one exhales. Try to find the deepest part inside your heart. Tell it that you wish to clean it and make it beautiful. Ask yourself everyday, 'Am I getting better?' Just focus on that answer being 'Yes.' Focus on getting better each day by sticking to good habits of thoughts, feelings, and actions. Don't worry about the far-off future just right now."

3. "Open your eyes and update your Spiritual Heart Visual removing any vices that you have avoided and keeping any vices that you are still trying to improve. Do not despair if vices remain—your

intention is what matters!"

4. "Write down what you would like to improve and name at least one easy way that you can improve."

5. If possible, offer one-on-one time with each child to listen to their ideas and feelings about the class and daily activities, and reflect on their artwork.

Chapter Thirty-Four and Chapter Thirty-Five Curriculum Guidance

Core Lesson for Chapter Thirty-Four: Imam al-Ghazali uses the metaphor of camels on a journey to underscore the idea of being prepared for one's own spiritual journey. Our bodies, which carry us the way camels do, need physical and spiritual nourishment. There is also no point in studying how the spiritual heart is cleansed if we don't bother to make the journey. Our low doings are like rocks along the way that must be overcome. The treasure trove of Real Learning must not be squandered or wasted.

Essential Question for Chapter Thirty-Four: Can I be brave enough to go on this journey, and step over the rocks? What are some of my own difficult "rocks" I am having trouble overcoming?

Activity 1: Camel Game

Make some "rocks" from boxes and label each with something that's hard to do, like sharing or being patient. Then pretend to be a group of camels and when you walk up to each "rock," discuss among yourselves the difficulties these "rocks" introduce in each of your lives.

Core Lesson for Chapter Thirty-Five: People copy one another. So even if we pass along important and true ideas by what we say, it is only by doing them that we are worth being copied. Imam al-Ghazali left us with a careful map containing a step-by-step way to deeply grasp the meaning of Islam.

Essential Question for Chapter Thirty-Five: What am I teaching others by my actions?

Activity 1: Connecting to the Quran

Read to the children Surah 67 verses 1–2 and reflect upon its meaning:

"Blessed be the One in Whose hands is sovereignty: and He has power over all things—He Who created death and life that He may test which of you is best in deeds And He is the Almighty, the One Who is Ever Ready to Forgive."

Activity 2: "How Silly?" Demonstration

Schedule an outing with the children that you will truly take. For example, a picnic in which the children will need to pack their lunches and supplies. Ahead of time, ask the children to make a list of all the things they will need for the outing and then to pack everything. Right before you leave, ask your children what they would say if you decided not to go on the outing. Sit down, and give them time to answer and think about what a waste all of their preparation was if they do not actually take the trip. Point out that learning religious knowledge, and then failing to act on it, is the worst waste of all. You could complete the other activities in this section at the picnic for a change of scenery.

Activity 3: Be Courageous! What Would Allah ﷻ Want Me To Do? Game

Based on the number of children attending your class, prepare at least one developmentally appropriate scenario for each child. The scenarios should narrate a conflict in which the children will have to have courage to do the right thing. After reading the scenario, ask the child to answer, "What would Allah ﷻ want me to do?"

Here are a few scenarios for example:

1. You just made friends with the most popular girl at school, and she told you she is going to ask

her mom if you can come over to her house this weekend to play. You feel so special and happy because only very popular kids get to come over to her house to play. At recess, you are playing together when she starts to throw rocks at a girl sitting in the corner of the play yard all by herself.

2. Your brother is playing a game with his friends, and they tell you that they don't want you to play with them. You feel sad and walk away when you remember that you know an embarrassing secret about your brother.

3. *Special* Responding to Islamophobia: Some boys in your neighborhood throw dog feces or pork at your doorstep, and shout insults about your Beloved Prophet Muhammad ﷺ. (Guide the children to see that it is their responsibility to respond in a peaceful and productive manner. Consider a special day just to focus on how to respond to Islamophobia in peaceful and productive ways.)

Activity 4: *Reminder* Serve Like the Prophet Muhammad ﷺ

This is a friendly reminder to keep up the group charity projects scheduled on your Good Habit Calendar such as feeding the poor or visiting the elderly/sick. Remind the children to stay positive, put others before themselves, and TRY TO KEEP SMILING just like the beautiful smile of the Prophet Muhammad ﷺ! To put everyone in a light mood, have the children pair off for "smile contests"—whoever can smile the longest at another person wins a treat. (Hint: Let everyone win a treat in the end so that the children's spirits remain high.) Provide options to help the children handle any difficult feelings that come up such as one-on-one time with an adult mentor, quiet time, or ability to change activities.

Activity 5: Secret Virtue Box

After allowing the children some time (recommended two weeks if possible) to practice their virtue, offer the Secret Virtue Box to each child so that a new virtue may be chosen, read, and noted, and then the slip of paper returned to the container. Remind the children of the Pearls of Wisdom, and talk positively to them about their efforts so far. You may choose to provide healthy treats around this time to make it pleasurable.

Chapter Thirty-Six Curriculum Guidance

Core Lesson: Life may be explained as a spiritual ascent to a higher and more Divine Knowledge and state of being. Imam al-Ghazali explains the three selves and how awareness of these provides some needed tools to help purify our hearts. Not understanding these three selves, many misidentify and imagine themselves to only be the lower self-centered egoist self and do not identify with their true luminous selves. This misidentification accounts for much great sadness and despair in the world. Understanding the three selves provides a tool—which can be used every moment—for the transformation of character and alignment with innate human dignity.

Essential Question: Do I want to know my true self? Or is knowing my lower self enough?

Activity 1: Connecting to the Quran

Read to the children Surah 50 verses 31–35 and 37. Reflect upon its meaning:

"And Paradise will be brought near to the God-conscious, no longer will it be distant: 'This is what was promised for you—to everyone who would turn to God and keep Him always in remembrance—Who stood in awe of the Most Compassionate though unseen and brought a heart turned in devotion (to Him): Enter here in peace and security; this is the Day of Eternal Life!' There will be for them there all that they may wish and yet more in Our Presence…In this, behold, there is indeed a reminder for everyone whose heart is wide awake—that is, who listens and witnesses…"

Activity 2: God Loves Me Circle

Preferably done after reflecting on the above verse of the Quran, sit in a "circle of remembrance" with the children and ask them to go around allowing each child to share one or more ways he/she knows that Allah ﷻ loves him/her. They can follow a format in speaking such as, "I know Allah ﷻ loves me because…Al-hamdulilah!"

Allowing the children to answer freely will give you a glimpse into their inner life so that you can better connect with them.

At first the children might focus on material life such as, "I know that Allah ﷻ loves me because He provides all of my needs for me. Al-hamdulilah!" If your group is mature, you might ask the children to reflect deeply again on the above verse of the Quran. Ask, "Why do our parents want us to become the best people possible? Now, why do you think God wants us to become the best people possible?" Allow discussion and more questions as necessary in order for the children to realize that a major proof of Allah's ﷻ love for us is that He wants us to become the best people we can become (just like the way parents want the best from their children). One of the children or you can say, "I know Allah ﷻ loves me because He wants me to be my best self and will reward me with a wonderful life now and forever! Al-hamdulilah!"

Activity 3: My True Self Craft(s)

Suggested materials:

    Poster boards
    Construction paper
    Glue
    Scissors
    Tape
    Colored pencils, markers, crayons, etc.
    Stickers

Open art: Provide a wide range of art supplies to the children, and ask them to be creative in designing an artistic representation of the three selves.

Charts: Ask the children to make two charts. The first chart will be entitled "The Lower Self—An-Nafs al-Ammara bi-l-su" and the second chart will be entitled "The True Higher Self—An-Nafs al-Mutama'inna." If you like, add a picture of the child on the chart that is "The True Higher Self." Ask the children to list actions that belong to the lower self and those actions that belong to the higher self. The charts can be filled in gradually. If your child has been behaving well, you may also encourage them by crossing out an action they used to do from "The Lower Self" chart.

Activity 4: The Three Selves Skit

Break up the children into groups of three. Ask them to develop a skit in which each person plays one of the three selves. Share the skits with the class. Optional: Record the skits or take pictures to include in later events celebrating the children's work. Please send these to be posted on www.ghazalichildren.org if you can.

Activity 5: The Three Selves Walk

Similar to the "Journey of My Life Walk" in Chapter Thirteen, this activity includes a group walk with three distinct right turns. First meet with the children in a huddle and let them know that they are going to learn how to watch the conversations that go on inside of themselves. Going on a walk is an excellent way to spend time on self-reflection.

Ask them to think about something that is bothering them. Maybe a boy worries that his little sister is getting all the attention at home. During the first segment of the walk, they will "watch the conversation" of their lower selves, allowing themselves to repeat the usual negative things they say in their minds. After five minutes, plan to make a right turn and then instruct them to "watch the conversation" of their scolding self, allowing themselves to repeat the usual self-correcting things they say in their minds, like "But she is little and *needs* more attention."

After five minutes, plan to make another right turn and then instruct the children to try to quiet all talking in their minds. Tell them to ask themselves, "What does Allah ﷻ wish of me?" Answering this question can come from the true self. "Be at peace. No need to be jealous. Love what you have been given."

Activity 6: The Courtyard Game

On a sunny day, take the class outside. Let each child gather enough sticks that can be made into square shapes on the ground, large enough for the child to sit inside. (If no sticks are available, the teacher can bring 4 long strips of string instead, each being 4 feet long, per child.) When everyone is seated, ask them to pretend that the sticks or strings represent walls which surround their personal courtyards, back gardens or patios at home.

Ask each child to describe what his or her walls are made of. Pretend that these walls are the things that make each person different from and separate from everybody else. A wall is made up of preferences that are particular to each person e.g." I have a cat named fluffy." "I love to play baseball." "I don't like spinach." " I am good at math." "I live near a lovely park." And so on. When the children have all described their individual likes, dislikes and lives, ask them to look at up the sun. Explain that if one symbol for God is the sun, and the Light of the Sun falls equally into each of our courtyards and is the *same* Light, then we are only separated by the walls of our different stories.

Now ask the children each to explain how something in their "walls" could be a part of their lower selves-like pride at being the best in some sport. Finally ask them which of their three selves prefers the Light in the center of their courtyards. Let everyone shut their eyes and imagine that their inner Light is the same as their classmates. Ask them to imagine that though each of them looks different, the heart is the same one.

Activity 7: *Special* Spiritual Heart Check-In with *Dhikr* and Update Spiritual Heart Visual

Ask the children to spread out in the classroom with their journals and spiritual heart visual craft and answer your guided questions to themselves. The environment should be serene to enhance personal reflection.

Tell the children you are going to share a special *hadith* with them, with a cure for any difficulties they have been facing in purifying their spiritual heart. Rasul Allah ﷺ said: "Whoever says 'Subhaanallahi wa bihamdihi (Glorified is Allah and praised be He)' one hundred times a day, will have his sins forgiven even if they are like the foam of the sea." (Bukhari and Muslim).

Ask the children if they could say this *dhikr* one hundred times, and to notice how they feel.

Remind the children to also update their Spiritual Heart Visual.

Chapter Thirty-Seven and Chapter Thirty-Eight Curriculum Guidance

Core Lesson for Chapter Thirty-Seven: Imam al-Ghazali explains that if you want either worldly riches or Real Learning you need first to find the source of each and then find the way of gaining that wealth or knowledge. Wealth can be shared and does great service for the needy, but spiritual learning shared by being an example of it is more noble. Sharing the lasting treasures of Heart Knowledge can help others to discover their real true selves and enter Paradise in the next world.

Essential Question for Chapter Thirty-Seven: Which is more important to me, worldly riches or Real Learning? Why?

Core Lesson for Chapter Thirty-Eight: Imam al-Ghazali explains that when we teach others we must treat everyone as though they were our children or our family by being examples of mercy and compassion. Imagine everyone in the world is our family. The children now understand that there are those who will be greedy and brag because they do not realize that life is not for owning more and more, but instead, for being pure and serving others. There is no race to beat anyone in polishing one's heart. The children realize their bodies need care because they have been given bodies so that their hearts can ride inside them during the time needed for polishing.

Essential Question for Chapter Thirty-Eight: Who am I racing against in my life and trying to beat?

Activity 1: Connecting to the Quran

Read to the children Surah 9 verse 71, and reflect upon its meaning:

"As for the faithful, both men and women—they are protectors of one another: they urge the doing of what is right and forbid the doing of what is wrong, and are constant in prayer, and render the charity that purifies, and they heed God and His Messenger. It is they on whom God will bestow His blessing: truly, God is Almighty, Truly Wise."

Activity 2: Love Our Teachers Day

Children tend to enjoy brainstorming the ideas to accomplish a task. Ask the children to come up with a way to show appreciation for their teachers. Ask them to incorporate a passage from one of the beautiful *hadith* or Quran which they have learned about teachers. For example, the Prophet Muhammad ﷺ said, "In truth Allah and His angels as well as the heavens and the earth, even the ant in its hill and the whale in the sea, will bless the man who teaches his fellow men," (Tirmidhi). They could draw a picture of this. The children can honor their parents and/or teachers from school or elsewhere. Assist the children in accomplishing whatever feasible idea they decide on.

Activity 3: *Reminder* The Belongings of Paradise Charity Box

Schedule this day on your calendar so that the children are prepared and have chosen an item to bring into the classroom for the charity box. Remind the children something like, "While we do not bring any belongings from this life into Heaven, that's all right because the more good deeds we do in this life, Allah ﷻ will give us even better gifts and everlasting happiness in this world and Paradise."

Before the children put their donations into the box, ask them to remember using the item and how happy they felt at the time. Then ask them to explain why they don't use the item anymore. After they answer, explain to them again that these toys only bring happiness for a short period of time, but the actions that strengthen the spiritual heart will bring happiness in this world and the next.

Repeat this activity bi-weekly or monthly, and have the children take turns delivering the items to a chosen charity organization. We recommend that the children bring in only one item at a time so that they will have items to give in the future.

Activity 4: Secret Virtue Box

After allowing the children some time (recommended two weeks if possible) to practice their virtue, offer the Secret Virtue Box to each child so that a new virtue may be chosen, read, and noted, and then the slip of paper returned to the container. Remind the children of the Pearls of Wisdom, and talk positively to them about their efforts so far. You may choose to provide healthy treats around this time to make it pleasurable.

Chapter Thirty-Nine Curriculum Guidance

Core Lesson: A story about Omar who is "playing school" illustrates the humiliation and unhappiness that a thoughtless teacher can cause students through unkindness. This is no different than the misery any of us can cause one another through lack of manners, 'adab,' or gentle treatment.

Essential Questions: How do I like to be treated? Can I be strong enough to treat others that way?

Activity 1: Connecting to the Quran

Read to the children Surah 16 verse 125, and reflect upon its meaning:

"Invite (people) to your Lord's way with discretion and kindly instruction, and discuss (things) with them in the politest manner. Your Lord is quite Aware as to who has strayed from His path, just as He is quite Aware of those who have consented to be guided."

Activity 2: Hasan and Hossein's Winning Method

Share with the children the story of Hasan and Hossein (may Allah ﷻ eternally bless them) in which the two boys saw an older man making ablutions incorrectly. Instead of scolding him, they asked him to watch each of them make *wudu* and be a judge as to who made *wudu* the best. In this way, the man realized his own mistakes and was not offended. Ask the children to act out this scenario, or come up with different ways in which they could gently teach someone who was doing something incorrectly.

Activity 3: Open Microphone Assignment

One way to bring closure to the Book of Knowledge from the Ghazali Children's Series is to end with a story-telling/poetry/art ceremony. Ask the children to write a short story or poem or create a piece of art that demonstrates an important lesson they have learned in this Series. Let the children know that at the next meeting you will be celebrating the end of Book One and inviting guests to witness the closure ceremony. More ideas for the final chapter and closure ceremony are found in Chapter Forty Curriculum Guidance.

Activity 4: *Reminder* Serve Like the Prophet Muhammad ﷺ

Smile please! This is a friendly reminder to keep up the group charity projects scheduled on your Good Habit Calendar such as feeding the poor or visiting the elderly/sick. Remind the children to stay positive, put others before themselves, and TRY TO KEEP SMILING just like the beautiful smile of the Prophet Muhammad ﷺ! To put everyone in a light mood, have the children pair off for "smile contests"—whoever can smile the longest at another person wins a treat. (Hint: Let everyone win a treat in the end so that the children's spirits remain high.) Provide options to help the children handle any difficult feelings that come up such as one-on-one time with an adult mentor, quiet time, or ability to change activities.

Activity 5: Guided Personal Reflection and Update Spiritual Heart Visual

Ask the children to spread out in the classroom with their Spiritual Heart Visual craft and/or journals. Ensure a serene environment perhaps with soft Islamic songs playing in background.

Provide a coloring sheet with one of the 99 Names ﷻ written in Arabic calligraphy. When beginning the reflection, the children can color this Name ﷻ. http://freecoloringpages.co.uk/?q=99%20allah%20names

Interchange coloring with free-drawing or other forms of art in future repetitions of this activity. (Ask the children to draw something that appealed to them in the lesson and to share the meanings behind their artwork later.)

Suggested Script:

1. Ask the Essential Question(s) of the chapter to the children, and allow them time to ponder upon their answers with their eyes closed or write it out in a personal journal.

2. Softly and kindly say something like this to the children: "Now close your eyes and focus on breathing in and out for 7 breaths repeating 'Al-' as one inhales and 'Hamdulilah' as one exhales. Try to find the deepest part inside your heart. Tell it that you wish to clean it and make it beautiful. Ask

yourself everyday, 'Am I getting better?' Just focus on that answer being 'Yes.' Focus on getting better each day by sticking to good habits of thoughts, feelings, and actions. Don't worry about the far-off future just right now."

3. "Open your eyes and update your Spiritual Heart Visual removing any vices that you have avoided and keeping any vices that you are still trying to improve. Do not despair if vices remain—your intention is what matters!"

4. "Write down what you would like to improve and name at least one easy way that you can improve."

5. If possible, offer one-on-one time with each child to listen to their ideas and feelings about the class and daily activities, and reflect on their artwork.

Chapter Forty Curriculum Guidance

Special Note: This chapter may be taught as its own chapter with a separate closure ceremony or as part of the closure ceremony. The below activities are also part of the curriculum for Chapter Six so you might also think about saving some of them for this occasion.

Core Lesson: Omar tells a story which demonstrates what a good teacher should be like and how children can be good teachers too . One practices the *sunna* of the Prophet ﷺ by being always merciful, never speaking badly of another, avoiding envy, greed, arguing, pride, lying, sloth, and hypocrisy. If what we 'know' is not our 'state of being,' it's just so many words.

Essential Questions: How would you behave if you were in the company of the Prophet Muhammad ﷺ? Can you try to act that respectful way today with others? Show what that is like.

Activity 1: Connecting to the Quran

Read to the children Surah 13 verse 11 and reflect upon its meaning:

"God will not change the condition of a people until they change what is within themselves." Ask the children to reflect specifically upon what has changed in their lives since beginning to work on good character and on purifying their spiritual hearts? How can changing what's inside of us change the way we grow, just like the two trees?

Activity 2: Ceremonial Tree Planting

A ceremonial tree may be planted in remembrance of the special class you have just completed. As this newly planted tree is just beginning its life, so are each of the students who have worked hard to learn how to grow into virtuous servants of Allah ﷻ. Reach out to families of the children, community members, or your local City Hall to ask if anyone would like and permit the children to plant trees on their property. Permission for one tree is sufficient, but the more the better allowing each child to plant a tree.

Vegetable seeds can also be planted if trees are not possible. For families that have the capability, allowing the child to plant a tree or vegetable seeds in their own yard would give the child the possibility of developing a habit of caring for the plant as it grows by watering it, propping it up, and removing any weeds.

Explain to the children that the plant needs to have good soil and clean water, correct propping, and removal of any weeds in order to grow and produce food, God-willing ﷻ. Emphasize that the good ideas they are learning are like the seeds, and they need to take care of them just like the plants in order to produce the fruits of good character. Nourishing oneself with real knowledge, performing good deeds, removing bad habits, and remembering Allah ﷻ much will make them grow into good people with beautiful characters.

Activity 3: The Blessed Tree Film

Refresh the children's spirits with this astounding film about a miraculous tree which loved the Prophet Muhammad ﷺ. It can be downloaded at this link for a reduced price:

http://www.tenthousandfilms.com/The_Blessed_Tree.html

Questions for children about the film:

1. Why did the tree grow to become so strong even in the harsh desert?

2. How can love of the Prophet Muhammad ﷺ help you to grow into the best person possible?

Activity 4: My Growing Tree Craft

Suggested materials:

Durable sheets of construction paper, cardboard, etc.
Markers
Paste
Scissors
Cut-outs of trees, leaves, and fruits from durable craft materials mentioned above
Small drawings illustrating good virtues (can also be written out)
Small drawings representing good fruits which arise from virtuous habits. For example, happy faces; a picture of poor children being fed and smiling; a picture of a child with his parents smiling at the child proudly. These ideas could also be written out in words.

Each child is asked to draw a bare tree with many roots and leafless branches reaching Heavenwards. The teacher could offer a cut-out that could be traced.

Children can paste drawings, pictures, or words of good habits on the roots. These are things that would grow into beautiful trees, like those mentioned in Chapter 6, such as "Memorize Quran," "Make Five Daily Prayers," "Honor Elders," "Be Truthful" etc.

Now decorate the tree with leaves and fruits using markers or paste cut-outs of leaves and fruits made from a durable material.

Finally, write words or paste pictures and drawings of the "good fruits" that will come from their virtuous habits onto the tree limbs.

Closure Ceremony Guidance

Activity 1: Open Microphone Storytelling

Arrange a stage with a real or pretend microphone and seating arrangements for invited families, teachers, and friends. Each child will have their turn at the microphone to read their story to the audience showcasing an important lesson they have learned during this Series.

Activity 2: Award Certificates

Create or purchase formal award certificates for the children. It may read something like, "Congratulations Fatima Shah for your hard work completing the Book of Knowledge from the Ghazali Children's Series. May Allah ﷻ guide you always. Ameen."

Activity 3: Islamic Song Concert

Along with the storytelling, the children can share the spirit of the lessons they have been learning by singing the Islamic songs for their parents, teachers, and friends.

Activity 4: Memory Lane

Collect all the photos and recordings taken of the children during class time and community service projects. Print the photos to be displayed at the closure ceremony or create a picture slide show with a beautiful Islamic song playing in the background.

Activity 5: Parting Blessings

Ask a respected elder or scholar in your community to join the ceremony in order to make the final parting words and say a *du'a'* for the children and their families.

This publication was made possible through the generosity of international donors and through the support of a grant from the John Templeton Foundation. The opinions expressed in this publication are those of its authors and do not necessarily reflect the views of the John Templeton Foundation.

Fons Vitae would like to thank the entire team of children, teachers, and parents who worked to develop the Curriculum Guide. Bless Pari Ansary, Marwah Helmy, Sarah and Jennah Abid, Suzzane Muir, Siraj Mowjood, Mariam Hussain, Farkhandah Faraz, Sana Syed, Nimah Nawwab, Razwan Ul-Haq, Uzma Hameed, Tammy Elmansoury, Adam Shahrani, Sam Ross, and many others for their review of and contributions to this Parent-Teacher's Manual of Activities and Curriculum. May your reward be with Allah ﷻ. Ameen.